SEA AND AIR FIGHTING

SEA AND AIR FIGHTING

Those Who Were There

Edited by David Bilton

Pen & Sword
MILITARY

First published in Great Britain in 2016 by
PEN & SWORD MILITARY
an imprint of
Pen & Sword Books Ltd
47 Church Street
Barnsley
South Yorkshire
S70 2AS

ISBN 978-1-47386-705-5

Typeset by Concept, Huddersfield HD4 5JL.
Printed and bound in England by CPI Group (UK) Ltd, Croydon CR0 4YY.

Pen & Sword Books Ltd incorporates the imprints of Pen & Sword Archaeology, Atlas, Aviation, Battleground, Discovery, Family History, History, Maritime, Military, Naval, Politics, Railways, Select, Social History, Transport, True Crime, and Claymore Press, Frontline Books, Leo Cooper, Praetorian Press, Remember When, Seaforth Publishing and Wharncliffe.

For a complete list of Pen & Sword titles please contact
PEN & SWORD BOOKS LIMITED
47 Church Street, Barnsley, South Yorkshire, S70 2AS, England
E-mail: enquiries@pen-and-sword.co.uk
Website: www.pen-and-sword.co.uk

CONTENTS

LIST OF PLATES

The *Cap Trafalgar*, a German passenger liner converted to an auxiliary cruiser in the middle of August 1914.

The *Carmania*.

HMS *Audacious*, King George V-class battleship.

The RMS *Olympic*, lead ship of the White Star Line.

The crew of *Audacious* took to lifeboats and were rescued by RMS *Olympic*. The photo was taken by Mabel and Edith Smith.

HMS *Warrior*, a Warrior-class armoured cruiser launched in 1905.

HMS *Queen Mary* with her torpedo net booms folded against her side.

A German photograph showing the final minutes of the Battle Cruiser *Queen Mary*.

SMS *Frauenlob*, a German light cruiser sunk at the battle of Jutland.

HMS *Vindictive*, an Arrogant-class cruiser launched in 1897.

An aerial view of two British ships sunk in Zeebrugge harbour.

German heavy bombers taking off for a raid.

Manfred von Richthofen, the Red Baron, seated in the cockpit of the Albatross 111, with members of Jasta 11 in 1917.

Jadgstaffel 11 lined up ready for a patrol.

French troops on Gallipoli before an attack on 21 June 1915.

Some of the many wounded that were evacuated from Gallipoli and sent to Egypt or Malta to recover.

A BE2c (Bleriot Experimental), initially constructed for stability at a time when reconnaissance was considered one of the most important roles in aviation.

Hauptmann Oswald Boelcke, a German flying ace with forty credited victories.

INTRODUCTION

In the inter-war period many of the combatants on both sides wrote about their experiences in the trenches, at sea and in the air. Most of them have long been out of print and are difficult to find. This is one such book. These stories were first published in 1936 as part of a nearly 800 page book and are specially written vignettes from the writers' published books on their war. Some of the writers will be familiar to readers but most are little known.

The stories contained within this volume, one of three, are about the war at sea and in the air. What makes them special is that they were penned by the participants, some officers others merely soldiers, while their memories were still fresh and before their war – the 'war to end all wars' – had been replaced by another. Although their style may be old-fashioned they tell their tales truthfully so any editing has been kept to a minimum. Where possible the next pages fill in the background of the writers, putting them in a historical context allowing further research.

Contained within the pages of this book are stories of bravery and daring-do, on land, in the air and on the sea. Why a story about land warfare in a book about the navy and air force? Simple. The Royal Navy contributed men to form the 63rd Royal Naval Division which fought at Gallipoli and its ships had naval soldiers, the Royal Marines.

As well as fighting major battles with the German Fleet, the Royal Navy undertook other roles. They guarded convoys, swept the seas for mines to ensure the safe passage of ships from the continent, brought home wounded men, took men to war, fought on land with the army and fought the submarine menace using warships and Q ships. The fledgling Flying Corps started its involvement in the war as a tool for reconnaissance, quickly moving to armed combat and bombing. By 1916 a squadron no longer did everything, they had become specialised.

The stories by the famous and not so famous include Sir Compton Mackenzie, prolific author, writing about his experiences at Gallipoli and Commander King-Hall another noted author describing his experiences at the Battle of Jutland. E Keble Chatterton describes the duel between the *Carmania* and *Cap Trafalgar*, George Clark provides an eye-witness account of what was described as the greatest secret of the war and G Mulhauser explains how Q ships went about their work. The attack on the Mole at Zeebrugge is vividly portrayed by Captain Carpenter, VC and Alan Bott describes the daily work of the RFC in the early days of the war. Mrs Peel describes the bombing of the Home Front and the writer 'Vigilant' explains how the Red Baron met his end. Other stories include flying over the Western Front whilst hanging upside down and more about Q ships and their dangerous work.

ABOUT THE AUTHORS

Edward Keble Chatterton (1878–1944). A prolific writer who published around a hundred books, pamphlets and magazine series, mainly on maritime and naval themes. Born in Sheffield, he attended Sheffield Royal Grammar School followed by St Paul's School in Hammersmith, London. He took a BA at Oxford, before beginning to write theatre and art reviews for various magazines

A keen amateur sailor at the outbreak of the War, he joined the Royal Naval Volunteer Reserve, ultimately commanding a Motor Launch flotilla at Queenstown in Ireland. He left the service in 1919 with the rank of Lieutenant Commander and wrote about his experiences in *Q-Ships and their Story* (1922), *The Auxiliary Patrol* (1924) and *Danger Zone: The Story of the Queenstown Command* (1934). He also wrote a series of monographs on model ships, many narrative histories of naval events, a number of juvenile novels and books about boating on French canals.

George P. Clark. The Commander's Signal Yeoman on the super-dreadnought *Audacious*, sunk by a mine on 27 October 1914.

Gordon Campbell. One of seven OAs (Dulwich College pupils) to receive the Victoria Cross, Vice-Admiral Campbell was the successful commander of armed decoy vessels known as 'Q' ships during the First World War. In 1916 he was awarded the DSO for sinking a U-boat and a year later received a VC for successfully destroying another German submarine despite his own ship being hit and sinking. He became a Vice-Admiral in 1932. From 1931 to 1935 he was MP for Burnley.

William Stephen Richard King-Hall (Baron King-Hall) (1893–1966). A naval officer, writer, politician (MP for Ormskirk) and playwright. He served between 1914 and 1918, with the Grand Fleet, serving on HMS *Southampton* and with 11th Submarine Flotilla. He resigned from the navy in 1929 with the rank of Commander.

George Henry Pasche Mulhauser (1873–1923). Second-in-command and navigator of the Q ship *Result*. After the war he circumnavigated the world between September 1920 and July 1923. He died shortly after completing his voyage.

Commander Harold Auten VC, DSC, RD (1891–1964). Joined the Royal Naval Reserve (RNR) as an officer before the war. He was promoted to Lieutenant in 1917 and was awarded the Distinguished Service Cross 'for services in Vessels of the Royal Navy employed on Patrol and Escort duty'. His Victoria Cross was awarded for a Q ship action in 1918. Auten wrote *Q Boat Adventures* in 1919, the first book on the activities of Q-ships.

Vice-Admiral Alfred Carpenter VC (1881–1955). Selected by his fellow officers and men to receive the Victoria Cross after the attack on the Mole at Zeebrugge. He was in command of HMS *Vindictive* which was to land 200 Royal Marines for the attack. Carpenter retired from the navy in 1932 with the rank of Rear-Admiral.

Constance Dorothy Evelyn Peel OBE (*née* Bayliff) (1868–1934). An English journalist and writer, known for her non-fiction books on cheap household management and cookery. She wrote with the name Mrs C.S. Peel, taking the name of her husband, Charles Steers Peel. During the war she ran a Lambeth-based club for the wives of servicemen, and spoke on behalf of the United Workers' Association and the National War Savings Association. Peel co-directed, with Maud Pember Reeves, the women's service of the Ministry of Food during the voluntary rationing of 1917–18, as well as publicly speaking about economical household food practices. She was editor of the women's page in *The Daily Mail* after being appointed to the post in 1918 by Lord Northcliffe,

Vigilant. The pseudonym of Claud Walter Sykes, a writer who specialised in aviation books, including translations from German.

Sir Compton Mackenzie OBE (1883–1972). A prolific writer of fiction, biography, histories and memoirs, as well as a cultural commentator, raconteur and lifelong Scottish nationalist. He was one of the co-founders in 1928 of the Scottish National Party. Mackenzie was knighted in 1952.

Lieutenant Colonel L.A. Strange DSO, MC, DFC (1891–1966). Early English aviator who gained his licence in August 1913, afterwards taking a commission in the RFC. In May 1914, he was posted to the Central Flying School at Upavon. On the declaration of war he was posted to an active service squadron. Strange retired from the Service through ill health (sciatica) in 1921 and bought 1,300 acres of farm-land on the Isle of Purbeck. He served in the RAF during the Second World War.

Captain Alan John Bott MC & bar (1893–1952). A Great War flying ace who was credited with five aerial victories. He later became a journalist, editor and publisher who founded Pan Books. In early 1915, after training in the Inns of Court Officers' Training Corps he was commissioned as a second lieutenant in the Royal Garrison Artillery on 22 July 1915 but was later transferred to the Royal Flying Corps with the rank of lieutenant being appointed a flying officer (pilot), on 26 September 1916. Bott then trained as a pilot, being appointed a flying officer on 1 June 1917 and was posted to 111 Squadron RFC stationed in the Sinai Desert. He destroyed two enemy reconnaissance aircraft on 14 and 15 April 1918, but on 22 April he was shot down and taken prisoner by the Turks. He escaped to Greece, arriving there just as the armistice was declared. Bott left the RAF after the war, being transferred to the unemployed list on 18 February 1919.

CHAPTER ONE

AN HISTORIC DUEL

By E. Keble Chatterton

Our story begins at 8.00am on 7 August 1914, three days after hostilities broke out, and the scene is the Liverpool landing-stage, where *Carmania* had just arrived from across the Atlantic and was landing her passengers as quickly as they could step across the gangways; but then she was taken into dock to discharge her cargo, to coal, and fit out as an armed merchant cruiser. The change over from the character of a luxurious transatlantic floating hotel to a grim warship proceeded with amazing speed. Gangs of workmen were soon painting the red funnels black, shipwrights were cutting away bulwarks on one of her decks to allow guns to train round the necessary arcs; armour plates were placed over vital spots, rope protection to deflect splinters was devised, all woodwork between decks was stripped off, passengers' cabins put ashore for fear of fire, magazines built into the holds, speaking tubes installed to connect with the steering-room aft, eight 4.7-inch guns mounted, searchlights and a naval range-finder were fitted, and white upper works painted a dull grey. All this was completed within a week from the time of her arrival in the Mersey.

In the meanwhile her personnel had been provided, Captain Noel Grant, RN, being appointed by the Admiralty in command, with Lieutenant-Commander E. Lockyer, RN, as First Lieutenant. Her peace time master was Captain J.C. Barr, who was made Commander RNR. 'On the arrival of the ship at Liverpool from New York,' Captain Grant has related, 'I went on board and told Captain Barr that I had orders to commission the *Carmania* as an armed merchant-cruiser, that I wanted him to go with me, and I wanted the whole engine room complement from the chief engineer to the last joined trimmer. Captain Barr did not hesitate one moment. He said he would go in any capacity. He then sent for Mr Drummond, the chief engineer, who selected his officers and men, with the result that the whole department, without one exception, volunteered for the job.'

Several Cunard officers and a number of ratings remained, and a number of ranks and ratings from the Royal Fleet Reserve and Royal Naval Reserve arrived from Portsmouth, the able seamen being largely composed of those sturdy Scottish fishermen who did such magnificent work afloat in all manner of warships. A number of Marines also joined the ship's company. So on 15 August, with her bunkers full, a couple of naval semaphores showing up prominently, and her general appearance suggestive of an interesting warrior, the transformed *Carmania* went steaming down the Mersey, up the Irish Channel, across ocean to Bermuda, where she arrived on 22 August, coaled, and was next placed under Admiral Cradock's orders. She had taken every opportunity of dropping a target and doing some gunnery practice at sea, and the excellent firing had shown Captain Grant that his scratch crew would be likely to acquit themselves well if they ever went into action.

On 11 September, *Carmania* was ordered to intercept, with the co-operation of HMS *Cornwall*, the German collier *Patagonia*, which was about to leave Pernambuco, and had been working with *Karlsruhe*, but reached Bahia Blanca this month from Pernambuco, having evaded capture. *Carmania* was now given instructions to inspect that lonely Trinidada Island, which was being used as a raiders' base for coaling. Soon after dawn on 14 September *Carmania* sighted this lofty desolation sticking up out of the sea, and by 11.00am was able to make out the upper works of a large vessel lying in the western side. The day was bright and clear, and it was seen that the vessel had a couple of funnels. Now, that fact was significant. Was she a British man-of-war? Certainly not. Not one was in the neighbourhood. A British merchant ship, perhaps? Impossible. She would not have any reason for being at Trinidada. Obviously, therefore, this was a German. But who was she?

It may be said at once that neither then nor till several days afterwards was her identity known. She could hardly be *Dresden*, for the latter had three funnels; nor the *Karlsruhe*, nor the *Kronprinz Wilhelm*, each of which had four funnels. As a fact this was the Hamburg-South American liner *Cap Trafalgar*, a brand-new ship which had just been built with three funnels. One of the latter was a dummy and used for ventilation purposes, but had been got rid of. This luxurious ship of 18,710 tons and 17½ knots was not very dissimilar from the *Carmania* of 19,524 tons and 16 knots. *Cap Trafalgar* had reached Buenos Aires just before war began and at once became suspect: she was the very kind of craft that would make an excellent armed merchant cruiser.

The Argentine authorities had her searched, but could find nothing warlike on board.

It is true that she had 2,100 tons of coal on arrival, but her bunker capacity was 4,000 tons. After discharging her cargo at Buenos Aires, she sailed at 5.00pm on 17 August, and it was thought that she had taken 3,500 tons of coal as well as large baulks of timber for shoring up her gun positions: yet on reaching Monte Video she was again searched, when only 2,100 tons of coal and no warlike stores were discovered. She now bunkered, took in 1,600 tons and left on 23 August nominally for Europe via Las Palmas. This, of course, was pure bluff, for after leaving the River Plate she met at sea the German gunboat *Eber* which had come across from South Africa with the collier *Steiermark*, and received *Eber*'s armaments consisting of two 4-inch and six 1.4-inch machine guns. *Cap Trafalgar* had then cruised for a fortnight with the aim of attacking British commerce, though she had no success whatever, and in the meanwhile *Eber* reached Bahia on 5 September flying the German mercantile ensign. Commander Wirth was in command of *Cap Trafalgar*, but so frequently did he hear the wireless of British cruisers that he was frightened away from the trade routes.

For about a week this German raider had been at Trinidada when *Carmania*, a triple screw, turbine-driven, eleven-year-old vessel began to approach the island. The Cunarder had been seen, and the Hamburg-South American began to stoke up, smoke issuing from both funnels. Lying alongside the *Cap Trafalgar* were two smaller steamers, but before *Carmania* could raise their hulls on the horizon these two cast off and made respectively for the north-west and south-east.

Captain Grant had to display caution at first. Who knew but at the other side of Trinidada there might be lurking in ambush some German cruisers? Who could say that there was not a signal party ashore to semaphore which side of the island *Carmania* was about to pass? Captain Grant determined to keep any watcher guessing and steered for the middle of Trinidada, intending when close to go suddenly east. But, having discovered this big German liner, he decided to keep the latter to starboard and steered south-west. At 11.30am all hands that could be spared in *Carmania* were sent to dinner, *Cap Trafalgar* seemed inclined to run away, for when the second collier had left her side, the German liner hove up anchor, backed out from the land, then went ahead and followed the first collier that was already out of sight at the back of the island. (The latter was the SS *Berwind*, flying the 'Stars and Stripes,' having been chartered from United States owners.)

Carmania began to chase, but *Cap Trafalgar* now swung round to starboard and headed across about four points on the former's bow. The enemy was flying no flag, was painted grey, with red 'boot-topping', red funnels with black tops. She therefore had the appearance of a Union-Castle liner and might have been about to attack the South African route shortly, for she could have reached the St Helena neighbourhood in less than four days and done an immense amount of harm. *Eber* conceivably may have given some useful information as to this trade.

But in spite of her disguise *Cap Trafalgar* was too stockily built, too like such a steamer as *Berlin* to be anything except German. Smart she certainly was, for she had made only one voyage. Surprised she was likewise, for she must have expected to see a Cunarder anywhere save at Trinidada.

At noon *Carmania*'s crew were sent to general quarters, and the largest British White Ensigns were hoisted at both mastheads as well as at the staff at the stem. It was still a small matter of doubt as to whether the German was armed, so at 8,500 yards the Cunarder fired a shot across the other's bows, and only at the last minute did *Cap Trafalgar* run up the German White Ensign. From now the duel between two nearly matched liners began, and it was to be a fight to a finish. Flashes were seen fore and aft along the German's decks, and shells came shrieking over *Carmania*'s bridge to fall some 50 yards to starboard into the sea.

'Let him have it!' shouted Captain Grant, and three guns on the port side which would bear now blazed away. The first rounds fell short, but the range was soon found, and in order that the fourth gun might come into action Captain Grant ported a little. Some excellent gunnery ensued, practically every round being a hit. But one German shell had burst on *Carmania*'s starboard side, killing one of the gun's crew and wounding others. Hits were frequent on both sides, and next the German closed to 3,500 yards so as to bring her machine-gun into use. There came a shell which carried away *Carmania*'s fire-control and made it no longer possible to telephone ranges from the bridge to the guns. The German was shelling concentratedly on *Carmania*'s guns and bridge, in order to make the duel no longer possible. The danger was that the machine-gun fire might make the bridge quite untenable and thus throw into confusion the direction of the ship. Therefore

Captain Grant ported, and in turning away to starboard increased the range, brought the aftermost 4.7-inch to bear, so that for a few seconds five of the eight guns were engaging *Cap Trafalgar*. But the latter ported also, bringing the guns on her port side to bear.

By this time it was apparent that the German had a distinct list to starboard; she had also been on fire forward but this conflagration had evidently been put out. The aim of Captain Grant was now to sink his enemy by directing attack at the waterline, and of course the shells went through the steel plates with disastrous effect so that the Atlantic poured in rapidly. Now this kind of single-ship fight between combatants that had been created for peace and comfort, for safety and luxury, was inevitably bound to cause grievous damage to both parties: there is something painful in the situation of two such noble examples of shipwrightry being put to such intolerable tests. Still, war is war, and raiders had to be fought wherever and whenever found. Those of us who crossed the ocean in *Carmania* when she first began her voyaging, and remember how with a beam wind she was almost as sensitive as a sailing vessel, could not have imagined that she should ever have endured the terrific hammering of battle.

Ventilators, rigging, derricks, and boats were showing ugly scars; German shells had penetrated into the second class smoke-room, where a few weeks previously nothing more explosive than a soda-water bottle had ever been heard. In the petty officers' mess some rounds had fallen with damage to hammocks, beds and clothing, though happily not to human lives. In a single-ship contest a hundred years previously the decision would have been fought out at close quarters, but in this modern engagement between two crack steamers of rival companies the range never got less than 2,900 yards, or about 1½ miles. As the distance widened, it was very obvious that *Cap Trafalgar* had not gained immunity by having closed for the benefit of her machine guns: she was listing in a doomed manner.

A conflagration had broken forth in Captain Grant's sleeping cabin through the impact of a shell, though soon put out thanks to the arrangements made for flooding. But presently the flames below the bridge again broke forth, and there were no means of putting them out, inasmuch as the water main had been shot through. Thus the bridge became uninhabitable and blazed fiercely.

From now, therefore, *Carmania* had to be conned aft, and she was in considerable danger of becoming that awful phenomenon of a burning wreck. But her peace-time master, Captain Barr, who knew her well down to her smallest rivet, did remarkable work in this crisis. 'Captain Barr,' remarked Captain Grant, 'was of the greatest assistance to me during the action, and it was due to his initiative that the fire below the bridge did not extend to the next deck.' She presented a battered picture, with this holocaust forward, the decks around the guns knee-deep in expended cartridge-cylinders, the port side of her main rigging shot away and hanging in meaningless festoons, the wireless aerials all gone long ago, some of the ventilator cowls ridiculously ribboned, a huge hole gaping on the port side of the upper deck, where a shell in its travel had been turned upwards against the side of the wheelhouse and then had passed through the after-bridge. In so doing, steel rails and stanchions had been twisted like bits of wire, whilst everywhere about the decks were fragments of boats and davits in a medley of destruction.

As to *Cap Trafalgar*, the listing of this tall ship went from bad to worse. She was still shelling rapidly, but with decreasing accuracy, and widening the range till the distance was now about 5 miles. Captain Grant whilst realising that this was about the extreme radius of *Carmania*'s guns, kept his ship dead before the wind; it meant increasing the range still further, but it was necessary to prevent the bridge conflagration from spreading. The German was badly alight, too, enveloped in smoke, and was noticed to be heading back to the island. Her guns became silent, she stopped her engines, began to lower her boats, and this was the time for *Carmania* to cease firing like-wise; every effort aboard the Cunarder being concentrated on stamping out the raging furnace that threatened death to all.

In *Cap Trafalgar* another race against destiny was being made. Half a dozen boats had been lowered from her and got away; no easy evolution from a height of 70 feet, with the great hull listing as if to drop on the men any moment. Around 2 miles away still waited one of her colliers, an awed spectator of an historic occasion, so to her these escaping Germans pulled. And then, just ninety minutes after the first shot had been fired, the newly built *Cap Trafalgar* heeled her enormous sides over till she capsized to starboard, her funnels lapping the Atlantic, and she disappeared bows first with colours still flying. Her death-agony was impressive, and no sailor could fail to notice how this mass of 18,710 tons seemed for a period to hesitate, heave herself upright with bows submerged, then suddenly tilt at a worse angle till her stem came out of water before takin a final plunge into the deep. Nothing now remained except a few swirling eddies, the usual indefinite debris, and the small white dots of lifeboats rowing hard towards safety. The crew of *Carmania* crowded to watch in awed silence this dramatic passing of a fine ship. And then, as if to relieve feelings so long pent up, a cheer was raised both for a gallant foe and for *Carmania*'s victory.

Commander Wirth was among those of the Germans killed. Captain Barr, who was not aware of this, remarked on a later occasion: 'I do not know his name, but he is the only German I would care to meet; for he put up a very gallant fight.' And that was the general feeling of the vanquishers. *Carmania* was in a bad way herself, with severe wounds, nearly one quarter of her guns' crews and ammunition-supply parties now casualties. Fresh smoke was seen on the horizon, and it was thought this might be another raider: indeed, it has been stated that it was *Kronprinz Wilhelm* coming to aid *Cap Trafalgar*. That is not correct, for *Kronprinz* was not as far south, though she did receive wireless news of the action. More likely the smoke was that belonging to one of *Cap Trafalgar*'s colliers. At any rate Captain Grant, with his ship in a crippled tangle, well appreciated that *Carmania* was in no condition to fight another engagement. She had been hit by seventy-nine projectiles, and there were 304 holes in her.

All internal communications and all navigational instruments had been destroyed by the conflagration, and it remained for the commanding officer to get her away into safety as well and as soon as he could. He therefore proceeded full speed to the south, and at dusk altered course for the Abrolhos Rocks, which he reached in spite of uncertain navigation and having to steer the ship from aft. During the night *Carmania* got in wireless touch with HMS *Bristol*, arranged with her a rendezvous for the morning so that under the escort of this cruiser as well as *Cornwall*, the Abrolhos anchorage was attained by 8.00am. *Carmania* had steered to the south-west by the sun and north-east wind, until such time as some remains of the navigational gear could be fixed up. This is how Captain Grant describes the situation: 'When I first looked round after the action, I found we were in a very uncomfortable position, having no effective compasses, no charts, no chronometer or sextant or wireless code. The ship had to be steered from the after lower position, the only communication from the deck being a relay of men to pass the word down the engine-room skylight by blasts on a mouth whistle. I afterwards found that two midshipmen, Mr Coulson (who, I am sorry to say, was later on in the war killed in a submarine) and Mr Dickens, had gone out to the burning bridge and, at great personal risk, got the bowl of the standard compass, some charts, and the remains of the much-burnt wireless code. A sextant was found in a cabin between decks, so that by fixing the compass on a long pole, and deadening the vibration by placing it on a feather pillow, we were able to steer a moderately correct course, and we were very pleased to find our signals passing through correct enough to enable the *Bristol* to take us up the next morning, and escort us to a safe anchorage where we met other ships, and with their help we were able to make the ship seaworthy for the cross-Atlantic trip to Gibraltar.'

Cornwall's engineers helped to patch up her holes temporarily, some navigational instruments were borrowed, and on the evening of 17 September, escorted by that other armed merchant cruiser, *Macedonia*, *Carmania* started off for Gibraltar amid the cheering of *Cornwall* and two colliers. On the way north two days later she passed *Canopus*, whose people cheered her likewise. That same afternoon, the 19th, she touched at Pernambuco whence Captain Grant sent his despatches to the Admiralty, and nine days later arrived at Gibraltar where she underwent a long refit. She then was again commissioned as an armed merchant cruiser till she was returned to her owners in May, 1916. When war ended this wonderful ship was again put on the Atlantic passenger service as if she had done nothing else all her life. But the duel has now become a part of naval history, and as a distinguished Admiral (since dead, one of whose ancestors fought under Nelson at Trafalgar) remarked, there never was a single-ship action which reflected greater credit both on the Royal Navy and on the Mercantile Marine. Very aptly has it been compared with the fight between *Shannon* and *Chesapeake*. Both *Carmania* and *Cap Trafalgar* were well fought, well handled, and fairly well matched, though the German had better guns.

'The action,' says Captain Grant, 'was the only one throughout the war in which an equal, or as a matter of fact a slightly inferior, vessel annihilated the superior force.* My contention that we were the inferior vessel is based on the fact that the *Cap Trafalgar* was a faster ship and outranged ours by 2,000 yards. I am therefore thankful that the German Captain came in towards me and put up a perfectly fair fight, instead of taking advantage of the two great assets in a naval action. I shall always feel proud of the fact that it was my great good

---

* This is not quite accurate, cf. the fight between the *Dundee* and the *Renee*.

fortune to command a ship in action in which the glorious traditions of the British Navy were upheld by every soul on board.'

The total casualties were nine killed or mortally wounded, and twenty-six wounded. On Captain Grant and Captain Barr the King conferred the Order of the Companion of the Bath, whilst two of the crew received the Distinguished Service Medal. Had *Macedonia* whilst escorting *Carmania* met and sunk *Kronprinz Wilhelm*, German commerce raiding would have received another ugly blow, and fate might have so ordered the encounter had not *Kronprinz* remained in the Trinidada area till the end of September. But the destruction of *Cap Trafalgar* and discovery of Trinidada as a coaling base, together with the detention of so many supply colliers, came as a serious discouragement to the German Admiralty, who on 20 September sent out from Norddeich long-distance wireless station to one of their interned liners at Lisbon – and thence broadcast elsewhither – the information that all German coaling rendezvous had been compromised excepting possibly the spot where *Eber* had met *Cap Trafalgar*. Nauen sent this message to all German cruisers at sea, and thus increased their anxieties about receiving supplies.

Cap Trafalgar's survivors after having been picked up by the collier were landed at Buenos Aires, where they became interned. It was thus at last unmistakable evidence began to gather that the elaborate German Supply System was beginning to be broken up, not so much by British cruisers hunting the raiders as by trying to discover the latter's rendezvous, and by keeping a watch on ports where suspected supply ships were known to be and likely to break out. The weakness of Germany's raiding strategy, dependent as it was on the violation of neutral waters persistently, and on the secrecy of lonely rendezvous, became only too apparent after the first phase of war.

CHAPTER TWO

THE SINKING OF THE
AUDACIOUS

By George P. Clark

The sinking of HMS *Audacious* has been described as the greatest secret of the war. Manned by 1,000 picked officers and men, she was Great Britain's crack battleship and the pride of the British Navy. At exercises and gunnery, and for smartness and cleanliness, she could not be beaten, and for a ship to attain such a status as this in pre-war days was, indeed, a tremendous achievement, for competition in the Fleet was keen, and enthusiasm ran very high. It is, therefore, no wonder that when disaster befell this great ship and brought about her total loss, the Admiralty took most extraordinary precautions to keep the news from the Germans.

We, the officers and crew, were all sworn to silence, and the British Press, by reason of an appeal from the Board of Admiralty to suppress the news, had no alternative but to remain silent. But rumour soon spread round the country until the story that 'a whole battle squadron had been sunk' was being freely circulated. The true story did eventually reach Germany through the medium of American newspapers, for during part of the time the ship was struggling for her life, she was photographed by American passengers on board the White Star liner *Olympic*, that was standing by.

We belonged to the 4th Battle Squadron comprising the battleships *King George V*, *Ajax*, *Centurion* and *Audacious*, and which was under the command of Admiral Warrender, whose flag, at the time of the disaster, was flying in the *Centurion*. We had shared those cold, misty mornings in the autumn of 1914 with the remainder of the Grand Fleet, steaming up and down the North Sea waiting and watching for the German High Sea Fleet. But when the big action was eventually fought between the two great fleets the *Audacious* was not there. She, or her shattered hull, was safe in that part of the graveyard of Mr Davy Jones which lies about 19 miles N ¼° E of Tory Island, off the north coast of Ireland.

A short time before this disaster happened, the German High Command had decided to mine the entrance to the mouth of the Clyde in order to intercept, and, possible sink, a convoy of thirty-three troopships with Canadian troops on board which was expected about that time. The German armed liner *Berlin*, with Captain Pfundheller in command, was selected for this dangerous and deadly work. The *Berlin* was, accordingly, loaded up with mines, and Captain Pfundheller's instructions were to lay them athwart the Glasgow approach between Garroch Head and Fairland Head; or, in the event of this being impossible, the principal change on, or south of, the line Garroch Head-Cumbrae Lighthouse.

As early morning fogs are frequent on this part of the Scottish coast in the autumn, the German captain was advised to arrive at his destination at about 7.00am under the cover of such fog or mist as might be present. And so, under conditions of the greatest secrecy, the *Berlin* sailed from the Weser on 21 September 1914, with her cargo of death and destruction-dealing mines. On his arrival at night in the vicinity of the Firth of Clyde, after having been six days at sea, Captain Pfundheller, his ship cleared for immediate action, was quite unable to fix his exact position by cross-bearings as, of course, the flashing lights which help navigators in this difficult part of the British Isles were not working. In these adverse circumstances he found himself compelled to abandon his original intention and decided instead to drop his mines in a position 19 miles N ¼° E. of Tory Island. It was one of these mines which sank the *Audacious*.

It is interesting to note at this point that had the mines been laid in the position originally intended they could not have damaged the large convoy of Canadian troops as all these ships were, fortunately, diverted to Plymouth where they arrived safely!

The 4th Battle Squadron put to sea in the morning watch of 27 October 1914, and, at about 8.45am, the Admiral made a signal ordering the Squadron to alter course 4 points to starboard. We, the *Audacious*, were the third ship in the line and were, I believe, a little out of station when we came up to the actual turning point. We did not answer our helm as quickly as might have been expected, and as we were swinging round to the new course in the wake of the two ships ahead of us, there was a sudden dull explosion on the port side aft, and obviously considerably below the waterline. The ship immediately heeled over to port and the engine-room quickly flooded. Clouds of steam and smoke burst from the after funnel and up the main hatches, and it was feared that the men in the stokeholds and engine-room had suffered bad casualties. They were, however, unharmed and, despite the inrush of water, stuck to it until ordered to go on deck.

In spite of having been badly holed by a very effective German mine, I cannot recall that the ship showed great distress as an immediate result. By this I mean that there was really no great amount of trembling in her such as one might reasonably have expected from so great an explosion – a fact which points clearly to her very solid construction. The list to port soon began to get worse, although, as is usual in any man-o'-war on occasions like this, the watertight doors had been closed wherever it had been possible to get at them.

After the sinking by a German submarine of the British cruisers *Hogue*, *Cressy* and *Aboukir* in September, 1914, the Admiralty issued instructions that where a ship was disabled by mine or torpedo whilst in the company of other ships, she must be left to her fate. We were left to our fate!

About midday, the White Star liner *Olympic* hove in sight to the westward. When she was as near to us as her captain, Commodore Haddock, thought safe, she lowered some of her lifeboats. These with some boats from destroyers, pulled towards us and managed, by daring seamanship, to get alongside and take off all but about 200 officers and men. These officers and men volunteered to remain on board and stand by the ship. She was doomed, so that there was no object in risking more lives than was necessary, for no one knew when she might capsize or blow up. Attempts were made to take us in tow, but they failed. We were so waterlogged and at the mercy of the sea that towing was impossible.

During the first dog watch, the Captain decided to reduce our number to about twenty. It was getting dark and the hungry-looking seas were leaping over the ship, impatiently waiting to claim us. It all looked pretty hopeless! There was, besides the possibility that the ship might go down suddenly, the greater risk that the torpedoes and ammunition might break adrift below and blow us up. Some impression of the state of the sea might be possible when I say that at times one could see the bow and stem of a destroyer right out of the water, while her midships was supported on the crest of a huge wave. Our quarter deck was under water, the main decks forward were awash, and we had, by this time, a most dangerous list, so about 6.00pm the Captain piped 'Abandon Ship!'

Only the Captain, Commander, Navigating Officer and myself now remained on board. It was pitch dark, icy cold and, of course, wet. The sea was getting more angry and restless. The awful moaning of the swirling water below decks is unforgettable. At one time I saw what appeared to be boiling oil oozing up through the seams of the upper decks. We were labouring heavily, and all but finished.

The Captain, Cecil V. Dampier, and Navigating Officer were still on the bridge. The Commander, Lancelot N. Turton, and I were standing together on the break of the foc's'le. His eyes were wet with tears. He was about to lose the ship in which dwelt his whole sailor's heart and soul. I believe that up to this time he had hoped to save her. His great courage and endurance, his kindly manner and methods, had been well to the fore all through. He was a gallant commander, and he knew no fear.

At about 8 o'clock he told me to go round wherever I could, hailing anyone who might be left on board – perhaps disabled or hurt. I found no one. The Commander now told me I could go. I left him – still standing alone on the foc's'le – to endeavour to find a way of getting clear of the ship. Swimming was, of course, impossible. I looked all round for something to use as a raft. There was nothing! Everything movable had been swept overboard. I began to feel a little dazed when, on the port beam, and almost alongside, I saw a destroyer's whaler. I hailed her and her coxswain answered me. Brave lads, that crew! They might easily have been dashed to pieces against our gunwale.

I waited my opportunity, and jumped – or rather threw myself into her, and then I must have lost consciousness, for I remember nothing more until I came to with a basin of rum to my lips in the foc's'le of the destroyer *Ruby*.

We lay off the *Audacious*, now completely abandoned, until about 9.00pm, when she blew up and sank. To see the huge pieces of white-hot metal falling back from the dark sky after the explosion was a sight I shall not easily forget.

The only serious casualty which resulted from our being mined was caused by some of the falling debris killing a petty officer on board the cruiser *Liverpool* as she was standing off. Not a single man was drowned.

Superstitious people may be interested to know that I was born with a caul. I am not, myself, superstitious; although I did carry this caul, hung round my neck by a silver chain, all the years I was at sea! Two things remain impressed on my memory. Though I had been soaked to the skin and partially dried again several times, I suffered no ill effects. I cannot remember having felt any kind of fear for a single moment during the whole long day. I sometimes tremble now to think of going through such another.

CHAPTER THREE

THE SHIP WINS THE FIRST VC

By Gordon Campbell

The submarine menace was at its height, and we had visible evidence of this a couple of mornings after we were at sea. We were steaming past the south-west corner of Ireland, when, as the day broke, we sighted what we at first thought was a periscope, and at once got ready for action; but we then saw several more 'periscopes', and began to rub our eyes to make sure we were awake. Conning towers also appeared, and, of course, we knew something was amiss; but it was barely light, and it wasn't till we got close up that we found a ship had been torpedoed and sunk, and between twenty and thirty men were struggling in the water amongst pieces of wreckage.

Some died before we could pick them up, as the water was bitterly cold, but we were able to rescue about twenty, two Scottish engineers and the remainder Lascars. One of the engineers related how he had been saved through standing on a horse-box, and that when the submarine tried to take him prisoner he dived into the sea, preferring to take his chance by diving and swimming to the comparative comfort of a submarine. Four of the Lascars died soon after we got them on board, and I buried them at sea.

The problem now was that I had sixteen additional men on board, fourteen of whom spoke no English, and we might at any minute meet the submarine that had done the damage; in fact, for all we knew, he might be watching us carrying out our rescue work. Something had to be done at once, so I sent for the two engineer officers and told them our game and what they were to do in action. I had a look at the Lascars, who were shivering with cold and obviously not yet recovered from the shock they had already received. I decided, therefore, that no instructions were necessary, as they would make an ideal 'panic party' without any explanations or rehearsals! American destroyers closed us during the forenoon, and we were able to transfer our guests. We were never keen to meet survivors of sunken ships, if any one else was at hand to do the job, but otherwise it had to be done in the interests of humanity. In addition to the fact that they were a nuisance aboard, there was always a certain amount of risk in stopping to transfer them, and, as in so many cases, it was a choice of evils, we could either keep them on board, transfer them, or return to harbour with them. Something had to be left to chance, and I always got rid of them as quickly as I could.

On this occasion a submarine alarm was raised whilst in the process of transferring them, and the transfer had to be postponed whilst the destroyers chased around looking for periscopes. Luckily it was a false alarm.

We continued to carry out our old programme of steaming west each night and east each day, in the latitudes which ships generally used approaching the south coast of Ireland.

We had no orders about returning to harbour this time, and we all felt confident we should have another engagement before we did so. The usual reports of all sorts were received, much as has been described, and it seemed only a matter of time. We were very pleased with our ship, and we lived in luxury and comfort compared with the good old *Farnborough*; with the men under the poop, the accommodation was not so crowded, and I had a real cabin on the bridge, whereas in the *Farnborough* I only had a make-shift one, with one door, which was always the weather one, especially up the Gulf! The *Pargust* never having carried coal, we got into the habit of keeping her a bit cleaner externally than the *Farnborough*, still as a tramp, but of a more respectable type. Of course, we didn't overdo it, and had the necessary amount of rust marks and patches of red lead about the place. Masters no longer carried wives on board, so the lady and the baby had long since been paid off.

Our dummy gun caused much merriment during the cruise, as of course as Master I was keen on the gun's crew being 'efficient', and so in broad daylight the two bluejackets would be seen religiously polishing it and practising loading! It was not only the proper procedure, but it was a great thing at this game, when you were asking to be torpedoed, to keep every one's spirits up by any means I could think of.

On 6 June Truscott informed me we should see a submarine tomorrow. On enquiring how he knew, he said that a bird had flown into my cabin, and although it had never struck me particularly before, a similar thing had happened on each occasion of engaging a sub-marine – and sure enough the omen came true.

On 7 June, a nasty-looking day, there was a choppy sea, heavy rain, and thick weather; we were steaming east on our 'homeward' course, and at 8.00am, when we were in latitude 51° 50′ N and longitude 11° 50′ W, a torpedo was fired at us from the starboard side at close range, and we couldn't have avoided it if we had wanted to. It jumped out of the water, showing it was running shallow, and hit the ship practically on the water-line bang in the engine-room, making a 40-foot hole and bursting the after-bulkhead. The engine-room and boiler-room formed one compartment, and were at once filled with water, also No. 5 hold.

The alarm had already been sounded, and on this occasion there was no need to say 'Torpedo hit', as, in addition to the lesson learnt in Q.5, the explosion being so high up had made an extra loud crash, and the loungers had been warned that a 'hit' would be in place of the verbal order. The starboard lifeboat was blown to smithereens, only one little bit of wood, which stuck on the aerial, being left.

The helm was put to starboard as we were hit, in order to form a lee for the boats. I watched the panic party rushing to the boats in the latest approved fashion. The remaining one lifeboat and two dinghies were lowered and filled with the crew.

Hereford, after taking the Master's best cap, seized his beloved stuffed parrot, and like a brave Master was the last to leave the ship, except for the 'unfortunate' firemen who crawled out at the last moment. I also had to watch our defensive dummy gun being 'abandoned' without firing a shot, in spite of going through pantomimic performances of trying to 'load it!' The Chief found his engine-room already occupied with water, and had to take up a hiding billet again.

I happened to know that Smith was again the engineer officer on watch at the time, and took it for granted he was killed, when, to my immense astonishment, I saw him staggering along towards his 'boat station' within a minute of the explosion. He was drenched to the skin, and didn't appear to know what he was doing. I had him led quickly to the saloon and locked him up there, as being the safest and quickest way to get rid of him. When I saw him afterwards he hadn't any idea of what had happened, nor does he know to this day. He was standing in the engine-room by the starboard side of the ship when he heard the alarm sound; he just had time to wonder where the torpedo would hit us, when it suddenly became black and 'he was swimming in the water for hours.' His duty after being torpedoed was to join the panic party, and obviously his subconscious mind was leading him, trying to make him do it. It was a most extraordinary escape, as the main engines, which were farther away from the ship's side than he was, were knocked down, all the engine-room ladders and gratings were blown away, and it can only be assumed that he was blown clean up through the engine-room hatch. After months in hospital and having a lot of pieces of coal, steel, etc. removed from his inside, where they had been blown, he recovered. The man in the stokehold was blown to pieces, but the second stoker was the most fortunate of the lot, as he had just been sent on deck with a message.

To go back to the action: Hereford again went in charge of the boats. At first we could see no signs of the submarine, but as the last boat was shoving off at 8.15am, the periscope was seen watching us from the port side about 400 yards off. He turned and came straight towards the ship for his inspection. I glanced through my slit and saw the gun's crew in the forecastle lying as still as the deck itself – not a speck of a face to be seen. They knew nothing of what was going on beyond that the ship had been torpedoed and their duty for the time being was to pretend to be part of the deck. My admiration for them was intense, as although everyone else on board was concealed, yet the others were in places where they could anyhow breathe in comfort and move their muscles. The submarine, with only the periscope showing, came to within 50 feet of the ship and passed close to the boats. He then sub-merged altogether. This was at 8.25am. A few minutes later the peri-scope was again seen close astern and passing to our starboard side. Jack Orr was lying at the wheel, and I said, 'For goodness' sake, don't move!' He said, 'It's all right, sir; I'm a lifebelt,' and I saw he had pulled a lifebelt over the most prominent part of his anatomy.

The signalman and I had to do a treble belly-crawl this time; the first time as the submarine was passing astern, then, after inspecting our starboard side he returned again to the port side where the boats were; and again when he came up the starboard side. The boats with the wind and sea had in the meantime drifted to our port quarter.

At 8.33am the submarine broke the surface on our port side about 50 yards off the ship, but he didn't open his conning tower; and although one shot might with luck have disabled him, I preferred to wait a more favourable chance when the lid was open. I had complete faith in my crew remaining motionless. The submarine was parallel to the ship and pointing towards our stern, where the lifeboat was, with Hereford standing up in his 'Master's cap'. He knew I didn't want to open fire on a bearing on the quarter if I could help it, as my 4-inch gun would not depress far enough. He, therefore, with great cunning and coolness, proceeded to pull towards my starboard side. The submarine followed him round, of course taking a bigger circle.

By the time Hereford was on our starboard beam I could see from the bridge the submarine coming close up under our starboard quarter. His lid was now open, and an officer, presumably the Captain, was on top with a megaphone, apparently shouting directions to the boat and then giving orders down the conning tower. I never took my eyes off this officer: as long as he was up I knew I could withhold my fire. When the submarine was clear of the quarter, Hereford realised I could open fire at any minute, and started to pull towards the ship, his job being done. The boat's crew was starting to laugh at seeing the submarine being slowly decoyed to its destruction, and they had to be cautioned to remember that they were shipwrecked mariners and had lost everything – it would never have done for the crew of the submarine to see them laughing.

The submarine evidently got annoyed at seeing the boat pulling back as he started to semaphore, and a second man appeared with a rifle or Maxim. There was nothing more to wait for – two men were outside, and the submarine herself was abeam of us about 50 yards away – and so at 8.36am, thirty-six minutes after being torpedoed, I gave the order to open fire. At last the forecastle 'deck' were able to stand up, and, tilting their gun up, join with the remainder in a heavy fire. The first shot hit the conning tower, and shot after shot went the same way; it was practically point-blank range. A torpedo was also fired, but did not hit; it was really only fired as an after-thought, as gunfire on this occasion was available.

The submarine started to heel over to port after the first two or three shots. She was steaming ahead, but stopped when on my bow with a heavy list to port and oil coming out of her. She opened the after-hatch; a large number of the crew came out of both this hatch and the conning-tower, and held up their hands, and some of them waved. I took this as a signal of surrender, and at once ordered 'Cease fire'. But no sooner had we ceased firing when she started ahead again. The men on the after-part of her were washed into the sea. Although she was apparently done, I was obliged to open fire again, my ship being helpless, and to avoid any risk of the submarine escaping in the mist. It was lucky I had a gun on the forecastle, as for about half a minute it was the only gun that would bear.

The forecastle gun's crew must have felt some satisfaction at a reward for their long wait. The ship being totally disabled, I could not turn her to bring the other guns to bear, and it was not till the submarine herself got clear of my bow that the other could join in firing the last salvo. After a few shots an explosion took place in the submarine, and she fell over and sank about 900 yards from the ship. The last that was seen of her was the sharp end of her bow with someone clinging to it. From the time of opening fire till the time she sank was four minutes, thirty-eight rounds being fired altogether during this time.

Several men were seen in the water after the submarine sank, so the boats went to their assistance, and after a good pull to windward they were in time to save two, but I couldn't help smiling when Hereford reported: 'We've again got a sample of each.' As in our previous action, wireless signals were now sent out for help, for although we were in a far more stable condition than *Q.5* – as only the centre part of the ship was flooded – yet we had no engines and so were helpless. I of course informed Admiral Bayly of the action, and he sent us a wireless signal: 'C.-in-C. to *Pargust*. I congratulate you and your crew most heartily on your magnificent record, and deeply regret the loss of one of your splendid ship's company.'

The prisoners in the meantime were brought on to the bridge in the chart-room. The first brought in was an officer, who, in addition to being wet through and covered with oil, had been wounded in his hand. After asking him his name, he collapsed and was violently sick. I then asked him the number of his boat. He got up, stood to attention, and said: 'Sir, I am a naval officer and will not speak.' I said: 'Well, you're a brave man,' and sent him down for a hot drink and a shift of clothing. The submarine turned out to be *UC 29*, one of the minelayer class, and no doubt the explosion at the end was caused by one of the mines. It was a long way out for a submarine of this class to be, as the water was too deep for laying mines.

We lay inert with nothing to be done till 12.30, when the *Crocus* arrived, and in a very seamanlike and expeditious manner took us in tow and towed us for twenty-four hours. The Queenstown sloops earned a grand reputation during the war for the magnificent work they did in towing ships in addition to their other duties.

HMS *Zinnia* and USS *Cushing* also arrived and escorted the ship after the prisoners had been transferred to the former with a hurried note from me to the Captain about them. She then took them direct to harbour. The tow was uneventful, there being no immediate danger as long as the bulkheads held. All the armament had been concealed again, and we were ready for action, but with an escort such an event was unlikely.

We eventually arrived at Queenstown at 3.00pm on 8 June, and were towed up to the Dockyard. As this was the first time we had had the honour of being escorted by one of the American destroyers, I broke all my usual orders, and called all hands on deck to give three cheers for USS *Cushing* as she parted company off Roche's Point. In addition to being Allies, we had the great thing in common of being under the same Commander-in-Chief. Admiral Bayly came to meet us outside the harbour and to see what could be done, telling us we were a great asset to the country. At this time it was not known what damage had been done to the engines, and whether she could be refitted in a reasonable time or not, and I requested to be towed to Plymouth, as being a bigger yard I thought it would expedite repairs or the fitting out of a new ship. We were taken up harbour and placed alongside the dockyard for the night whilst the Admiralty were being communicated with. The following day approval came for us to go to Plymouth, and we started at once in tow of the tug. On the way around we, as was usual at sea, remained ready for instant action. I had been offered an escort, but preferred to sail without. I thought we made rather a good bait as, if attacked, the tug would have come alongside, taken off the panic party, and left us for the rest of the 'stunt'. We got there safely after a tow altogether of over 400 miles. The ship was dry-docked as soon as possible, and after all the water had been got out, it was found that the repairs would take so long that we got permission to pay her off and start again.

My official report had in the meantime been sent in. I had no difficulty in stating accurately the exact time of events, as Nunn was at the fire-control station and exchange on the bridge within hail of me and noted everything down as it happened; but when it came to remarking about the conduct of my crew, it became more difficult, as on the occasion of Q.5. One could only say the same as before, that it was a 100 per cent affair. Any one individual could have ruined the whole show, and it must be remembered that I wasn't over-staffed with officers, and even if I had been it wouldn't have helped much had some individual given the show away. For instance, the men who formed the forecastle 'deck' – had one man moved an inch he would have spoilt the whole show, and it takes a little doing to lie motionless, as they had to, after the ship was torpedoed, for thirty-six minutes.

It may appear that the men in the boats had a fairly 'quiet' number, after they had merely run the risk of being torpedoed; but this was not the case, as I had always told them that the chances would be that the submarine would make towards the boats, and I might find it necessary to open fire when it was actually amongst them, and on this occasion the lifeboat didn't miss it by much. Had the two men on the conning tower showed any suspicion and gone below, I should have been obliged to open fire with our own men in the line of fire. They knew it, and not only never wavered, but, as already mentioned, had to be reprimanded for being too light-hearted.

We were indeed fortunate in only having one man killed by the torpedo, a very fine fellow, Stoker Petty Officer Isaac Radford. After our arrival at Plymouth we were able to bury him with naval honours. Smith had a narrow squeak. Not only did he come out alive, but his pig-headed Scotch (*sic.*) blood got him over his sufferings and he served again before the war ended. Admiral Bayly summed my crew up by saying that they had shown a 'disciplined and most efficient loyalty in *Farnborough* and *Pargust*, have been twice torpedoed, and are a great asset to the country.'

I was ordered to convey to the officers and men under my orders the Admiralty's 'high commendation of the admirable discipline and courage shown by them in this encounter, which will stand high in the records of gallantry of the Royal Navy.' The ship, as before, was also awarded £1,000.

The greatest honour of all was awarded the ship by HM the King, when he approved of one Victoria Cross being awarded to an officer and one to a man of HMS *Pargust*, the recipient in each case being selected by the officers and men respectively, in accordance with Clause 13 of the Statutes of the Victoria Cross.

This clause stated that 'It is ordained that in the event of any unit of our naval ... force, consisting in the case of our Navy, of a squadron, flotilla, or ship's company ... having distinguished itself collectively by the performance of an act of heroic gallantry or daring in the presence of the enemy in such a way that the Admiral ... in command of the Force to which such a unit belongs is unable to single out any individual as especially pre-eminent in gallant or daring, then one or more of the officers...seamen in the ranks comprising the unit shall be selected to be recommended to us for the award of the Victoria Cross in the following manner ... The selection to be by secret ballot ...'

This was indeed a very great honour, as it was the first time in the history of the Navy that a whole ship had been so honoured.

CHAPTER FOUR

THE BATTLE OF JUTLAND

By 'Etienne'
(Commander Stephen King-Hall)

In the battle of Jutland, I was by the chance of war placed in certain positions, at certain times, in such manner that in looking back on the action, I do not believe that a single observer could have seen more, except from an aeroplane. Most of the time I was engaged in taking notes, and it is of what I saw that I propose to write.

It may thus be accepted that, unless otherwise stated, the incidents described are facts for which I am prepared to vouch to the extent of my belief in my own eyesight.

On the afternoon of 30 May 1916, we were lying at Rosyth, and I was walking up and down the quarter-deck on watch when a string of flags rose from the *Lion*'s signal bridge.

I recognised it to be a steaming signal, and it turned out to be: 'Flag: *Lion* to Battle Cruiser Force and Fifth Battle Squadron. Raise steam and report when ready to proceed.'

We at once began to get the ship ready for sea. Our Sub-Lieutenant, one H.B. by name, was in the hospital ship close at hand where he had been sent to have his tonsils cut out. I had a curious feeling that we were going to have a 'show', and quite without authority I sent him this note in our steamboat:

DEAR H.B., I believe we are going out on a stunt, the steamboat is going to be hoisted, but if you want to come and can get away from the hospital ship, nip into her and come over.'

The Commodore had just come back from the shore, and I told him what I had done, and though he did not exactly disapprove, I saw that he thought it rather unnecessary.

When H.B. arrived, straight from bed – I believe he practically broke out of the hospital ship – our Fleet Surgeon was scandalised, and promptly ordered him to bed. I remember that I felt rather foolish when I went down to see him, and could only reply in answer to his enquiries as to how long the Huns had been out, that as far as I knew they were not out at all.

We sailed at 9.00pm.

The three light cruiser squadrons were up to strength, but the Third Battle Cruiser Squadron was at Scapa doing gunnery exercises; they were commanded by Admiral Hood.

We were reinforced by the Fifth Battle Squadron, consisting of the *Malaya*, *Warspite*, *Barham*, and *Valiant* under the command of Rear-Admiral Evan Thomas. The only other absentee was the *Australia* away refitting.

We did not know why we were going out, and to this moment I have never been able to find out officially what we hoped to do, but the *on dit* (a piece of gossip, a rumour – Ed.) was and still is, that we were to support an air raid or perhaps a mine-laying expedition in the Bight. At all events our immediate destination was a rendezvous near the Horns Reef.

The Germans stated after the action that their forces were engaged on an enterprise to the North.

I strongly suspect that this enterprise consisted in getting the British Battle Cruiser Force between their battle cruisers and battle fleet, for they knew very well that the region of the Horns Reef was a favourite spot of ours when we were making a reconnaissance towards the German Coast.

Everything points to the fact that for once they expected us there and laid their plans accordingly; or else they were out to do a raid on North Sea trade.

It will be seen how very nearly this former state of affairs material-ised, though it is impossible to assert definitely whether it was by accident or by design. We did not appear to be expecting Huns, as we cruised along to the eastward at no great speed; I think we were making good either 17 or 18 knots. At noon we received orders to have full speed ready at half an hour's notice, but as we were getting well over towards the Danish coast, this order partook of the nature of pre-cautionary routine. The order of the Fleet was the usual cruising for-mation by day. Course approximately east.

The battle cruisers were in two lines and close to them was the cruiser *Champion* and the attached destroyers. The seaplane carrier *Engadine* was also in company. Some 5 miles ahead of the *Lion*, the light cruiser screen was spread on a line bearing roughly north and south.

The squadrons were in groups of two ships, 5 miles apart, and the order from north to south was: First Light Cruiser Squadron under Commodore Sinclair, with his broad pendant in the *Galatea*; Third Light Cruiser Squadron under Rear-Admiral Trevelyan Napier, with his flag in the *Chatham*; and Second Light Cruiser Squadron, consisting of *Southampton* flying the broad pendant of our Commodore, the *Birmingham* (Captain Duff), the *Dublin* (Captain Scott), the *Nottingham* (Captain Miller).

Those of us who were off watch were dozing in the smoking-room after lunch, when the secretary put his head in, and said: '*Galatea* at the northern end of the line has sighted and is chasing two hostile cruisers.'

This was at 2.23pm and woke us all up with a jump.

I quickly went to my cabin and made certain preparations which I always did when there was a chance of something happening. These preparations consisted in putting on as many clothes as possible, collecting my camera, notebook and pencils, chocolate, and other aids to war in comfort in case of a prolonged stay at action stations.

At 2.56pm the *Galatea* reported that she had sighted the German battle cruisers, and we went to action stations, and the ship began to throb as we worked up to full speed. At about 3.00pm. we all turned to the NE to close the reported position of the enemy, who had turned from their original course of north to south.

As the northern edge of our screen only just made contact with the western edge of their screen, it will be seen how nearly we missed them.

The turn towards the north-east had brought us (Second Light Cruiser squadron) on the starboard quarter of the *Lion* and distant but 2 miles from her.

At 3.55pm the *Lion* turned to south-east and the battle cruisers assumed line of battle. This placed us before her starboard beam, and without orders we pressed at our utmost speed, followed by our three light cruisers to a position ahead of the *Lion*.

The First and Third Light Cruiser Squadrons, without signal, took station astern of the battle cruisers.

It was in these and subsequent movements without signals that the value was exemplified of all the exercises we light cruisers had done with the *Lion*. The light cruiser commanders knew exactly what Sir David expected of them, and they did it.

As the battle cruisers turned into line, I caught a distant glimpse of the silvery hulls of the German battle cruisers, though owing to the great range only parts of their upper works were visible for short intervals. They appeared to be steering a slightly converging course.

As the battle cruisers came into line, with *Champion*, her destroyers and ourselves ahead of them, both our own battle cruisers and the Germans opened fire practically simultaneously.

Our line consisted of the *Lion*, *Princess Royal*, *Queen Mary*, *Tiger*, *New Zealand*, and *Indefatigable* in the order named.

The Germans were almost entirely merged into a long, smoky cloud on the eastern horizon, the sort of cloud that presages a thunderstorm, and from this gloomy retreat a series of red flashes darting out in our direction indicated the presence of five German battle cruisers.

It was at once evident that though the Germans were but indifferently visible to us, we on the other hand were silhouetted against a bright and clear western horizon, as far as the enemy were concerned.

The German shooting, as has been the case throughout the war, was initially of an excellent quality. Our battle cruisers, about a mile away just on our port quarter, were moving along in a forest of tremendous splashes. Their guns trained over on the port beam were firing regular salvos.

At 4.15pm (approx.) I was watching our line from my position in the after control, when without any warning an immense column of grey smoke with a fiery base and a flaming top stood up on the sea, where the *Indefatigable* should have been. It hung there for I don't know how many seconds, and then a hole appeared in this pillar of smoke, through which I caught a glimpse of the forepart of the *Indefatigable* lying on its side; then there was a streak of flame and a fresh outpouring of smoke.

I turned with a sinking heart and watched the remaining five battle cruisers.

I can, nor could I next day, remember no noise. We were not, of course, firing ourselves, and it seemed to me that I was being carried along in a kind of dream.

I wondered what would happen next; each time the splashes rose on either side of the line of great ships it was like a blow to the body. We could not see from our low decks where the 13.5-inch shell were falling on that sinister eastern horizon from which the maddening jets of flame darted in and out.

At 4.23pm, in the flicker of an eyelid, the beautiful *Queen Mary* was no more. A huge stem of grey smoke shot up to perhaps 1,000 feet, swaying slightly at the base. The top of this stem of smoke expanded and rolled downwards. Flames rose and fell, in the stalk of this monstrous mushroom. The bows of a ship, a bridge, a mast, slid out of the smoke – perhaps after all the *Queen Mary* was still there.

No! it was the next astern – the *Tiger*.

Incredible as it may sound, the *Tiger* passed right over the spot on which the *Queen Mary* had been destroyed, and felt nothing. The time interval between her passage over the grave of the *Queen Mary* and the destruction of the latter ship would be about 40–60 seconds.

Just before the *Tiger* appeared, I saw some pieces of debris go whirling up a full 1,000 feet above the top of the smoke – it might have been the armour plates from the top of a turret. I remember that I found it impossible to realise that I had just seen 2,000 men, and many personal friends, killed; it seemed more like a wonderful cinematograph picture.

What did worry me was that we were now reduced to four. I remember saying to H.B., who had appeared from his sick-bed in pyjamas and a dressing-gown, though he subsequently put on some more clothes, 'At this rate, by 5.00pm we shall have no battle cruisers.'

He nodded solemnly, he was so hoarse he could only whisper.

'But,' I added, 'by the laws of chance one of them will blow up next, you see.'

We were by now right ahead of the *Lion*, and as I watched her, I saw a tremendous flash amidships, as she was hit by a shell or shells. I saw the whole ship stagger; for what seemed eternity I held my breath, half expecting her to blow up, but she held on and showed no signs of outward injury.

Actually, her midship turret, manned by the marines, was completely put out of action, and had it not been for the heroism of the major of marines the ship might have gone. He lost his life and gained the VC.

Soon after the *Lion* received this blow the Thirteenth Flotilla was ordered to make an attack on the German line.

It was extremely difficult to see the destroyers after they started, but I could vaguely see that they were coming under heavy fire as they got about half-way across.

It was during this attack that *Nestor* and *Nomad* were lost and Commander Bingham gained his VC.

At 4.38pm a very startling development took place. We suddenly saw and reported light cruisers followed by the High Seas Fleet bearing south-east. Sir David Beatty at once signalled to the Battle Cruiser Force to alter course 16 points (180°). This manoeuvre was executed by the battle cruisers in succession.

The German battle cruisers were doing the same thing at the same moment.

We disobeyed the signal, or rather delayed obeying it for two reasons: Firstly, we wished to get close enough to the High Seas Fleet to examine them and report accurately on their composition and disposition. Secondly, we had hopes of delivering a torpedo attack on the long crescent-shaped line of heavy ships which were stretched round on our port bow.

It was a strain steaming at 25 knots straight for this formidable line of battleships, with our own friends going fast away from us on the opposite direction.

As we got closer I counted sixteen or seventeen battleships with the four *König* class in the van and the six older pre-Dreadnoughts in the rear.

Seconds became minutes and still they did not open fire, though every second I expected to see a sheet of flame ripple down their sides and a hail of shell fall around us. I can only account for this strange inactivity on their part by the theory that as they only saw us end on, and we were steering on opposite courses to the remaining British ships, they assumed we were a German light cruiser squadron that had been running away from the British battle cruisers.

Only in this manner can I account for the strange fact that they allowed us within 13,000 yards of their line, and never fired a shot.

This theory is supported by the fact that when at 4.45pm the calm voice of Petty Officer Barnes on the foremost rangefinder intoned, 'Range one, three, five, double ho (*sic.*)! Range, one, three, two, double ho!' The Commodore saw that we could not get into a position for a torpedo attack, and as we should be lucky if we got out of the place we were then in, he gave the order for the turning signal, which had been flying for five minutes, to be hauled down.

Over went the helms, and the four ships slewed round, bringing our stems to the enemy. As we turned, the fun began, and half a dozen German battleships opened a deliberate fire on the squadron.

My action station was aft, but I could hear everything that passed on the fore-bridge, as I was in direct communication by voice-pipe. I heard the imperturbable Petty Officer Barnes continuing his range taking: 'Range one, three, two, double ho (*sic*.)! Range one, double three, double ho!'

Crash! Bang! Whizz! and a salvo crumped down around us, the fragments whisking and sobbing overhead. Suddenly I heard Petty Officer Barnes say, with evident satisfaction,

'Range hobscured (*sic*.)!'

I took a general look round, and the situation was as follows: About 3 or 4 miles north of us our battle cruisers were steaming along making a good deal of smoke and firing steadily, at what I imagined to be the German battle cruisers' distant hulls on our starboard bow.

Then came a gap of 2 miles, between the battle cruisers and the Fifth Battle Squadron.

These latter four ships had passed the battle cruisers on opposite courses when Sir David Beatty turned north, and as soon as they had passed him, Rear-Admiral Evan Thomas had turned his squadron to north by west, and followed up the battle cruisers.

It will be remembered that whilst this was going on we (Second Light Cruiser Squadron) had still been going south. When we turned to north, we found ourselves about a mile behind the last ship of the Fifth Battle Squadron. Our squadron was not in line, but scattered.

As flagship we had the post of honour nearest to the enemy. We maintained this position for one hour, during which time we were under persistent shellfire from the rear six ships of the German lines.

But we had them under observation, and we were able to transmit news of great importance to Sir John Jellicoe, whom we knew to be hurrying down from the north to our support.

We had experienced one shock to the system, on sighting the German Fleet right ahead, and we all anticipated that the Huns would shortly enjoy the same sensation.

The Fifth Battle Squadron just ahead of us were a brave sight. They were receiving the concentrated fire of some twelve German heavy ships, but it did not seem to be worrying them and though I saw several shells hit the *Warspite* just ahead of us, the German shooting at these ships did not impress me very favourably. Our own position was not pleasant.

The half-dozen older battleships at the tail of the German line were out of range to fire at the Fifth Battle Cruiser, but though we had gradually drawn out to 15,000–16,000 yards we were inside their range, and they began to do a sort of target practice in slow time on our squadron.

I was in the after control with half a dozen men, H.B., and the clerk. We crouched down behind the tenth of an inch plating and ate bully beef, but it didn't seem to go down very easily. It seemed rather a waste of time to eat beef, for surely in the next ten minutes one of these 11-inch shells would get us, they couldn't go on falling just short and just over indefinitely, and, well, if one did hit us – light cruisers were not designed to digest 11-inch high explosives in their stomachs.

The sub., who was practically speechless owing to his bad throat, and I agreed that we would not look at the Hun line.

But we could never resist having a peep about once a minute, and somehow we always seemed to look just as two or three of the great brutes flickered flames from their guns at us, and we knew that another salvo was on its way across.

We knew the time of flight was twenty-three seconds, and the sub. had a wrist-watch with a prominent second hand – we almost agreed to throw it overboard after three-quarters of an hour's shelling; at the twenty-third second the sub. would make a grimace, and as if in reply a series of splitting reports and lugubrious moans announced that the salvo had arrived. Frequently they were so close that torrents of spray from the splashes splattered down on the boat deck. Each shell left a muddy pool in the water, and appeared to burst on impact.

We all compared notes afterwards and decided that during this hour about fifty to sixty shells fell within 100 yards of the ship, and many more slightly farther off.

I attribute our escape, as far as we were able to contribute towards it, to the very clever manner in which 'I——', our navigator, zig-zagged the ship according to where he estimated the next salvo would fall. It was possible to forecast this to a certain extent, as it was obvious that the Huns were working what is technically known as a 'ladder'.

That is to say, the guns are fired with an increase of range to each salvo until 'the target is crossed', and then the range is decreased for each salvo until the splashes are short of the target once again. It is thus a creeping barrage which moves up and down across the target.

The best way to avoid it, is to sheer in towards the enemy when the groups of tall splashes are coming towards the ship, and as soon as they have crossed over and begin once more to come towards the ship, then reverse the helm and sheer away from the enemy.

The fascination of watching these deadly and graceful splashes rising mysteriously from the smooth seas was enormous. To know that the next place where they would rise was being calculated by some Hun perched up in one of these distant masts, and that he was watching those 'leetle (*sic.*) cruiser ships' through a pair of Zeiss binoculars – and I was watching his ship through a similar pair of Zeiss – was really very interesting. It would have been very interesting indeed if I could have been calculating the position of the splashes round his ship; but he was 16,000 yards away, and our gun-sights stopped at 14,500, so we just had to sit and hope we'd see the Grand Fleet soon. At 6.17pm the news that the Grand Fleet had been sighted right ahead spread round the ship like wild-fire.

Forgotten was the steady shelling – now we'd give them hell. The battle drew on to its dramatic climax when, faintly ahead in the smoke and haze the great line of Grand Fleet battleships became visible curling across to the eastward.

They had just deployed.

Then two armoured cruisers appeared from right ahead between ourselves and the German line. They were steering about south-west, and were moving in an appalling concentration of fire from the German battleships.

Whom could they be?

As I watched, the leading ship glowed red all over and seemed to burst in every direction. Our men cheered frantically thinking it was a Hun. Alas! I had caught a brief glimpse of a white ensign high above the smoke and flame, it was the *Defence* flying the flag of the gallant Sir Robert Arbuthnot.

The ship astern was the *Warrior*, and it was evident that she was hard hit.

The Huns redoubled their efforts upon her, when a most extraordinary incident amazed both sides. *The Warspite*, just ahead of us, altered course to starboard and proceeded straight for the centre of the Hun line. For some moments she was unfired at, then as she continued to go straight for the Germans the tornado of fire lifted from the *Warrior*, hovered as it seemed in space, and fell with a crash about the *Warspite*.

The *Warrior*, burning in several places, battered and wrecked, with steam escaping from many broken pipes, dragged slowly out of the battle to the westward; she passed about 400 yards under our stern.

Meanwhile with sinking hearts the sub. and I watched the *Warspite* and wondered what her amazing career portended. I focused her in my reflex camera, but so certain did I feel that she would be destroyed that I could not bring myself to expose the plate. I should guess that she reached a position about 8,000 yards from the German line when to our relief she slowly turned round, and still lashing out viciously with all her 15-inch guns she rejoined the British lines. At our end of the line there was a distinct lull. In fact, the speed of the tail of the Fleet become so slow that our squadron turned 32 points (a complete circle) in order not to bunch up on the battleships. In the course of this manoeuvre we very nearly had a collision with one of the Fifth Battle Squadron, the *Valiant* or *Malaya*.

It was now possible to try and take a general survey of the battle.

It was evident that the day of days had dawned, though too near sunset to suit us. At last the Grand Fleet and High Seas Fleet were up against each other, and the fate of nations was being decided.

For a seemingly endless distance the line of Grand Fleet battleships stretched away to the east. To the south, the German line, partially obscured in mist, lay in the shape of a shallow convex arc.

The Grand Fleet were loosing off salvos with splendid rapidity.

The German shooting was simply ludicrously bad, looking up our line, I sometimes saw a stray shell fall short of our battle fleet, and every now and then I saw a few fall over. Otherwise nothing anywhere near them.

I remember seeing the *Agincourt*, a few ships ahead of us, let off a ten-gun salvo – 'a truly Kolossal spectacle', as a Hun would say.

It was about now that I noticed that though the surface of the sea was quite calm, yet the ship was rolling quite appreciably. I then discovered that the whole surface of the sea was heaving up and down in a confused swell, which was simply due to the wash created by the 200-odd ships which were moving about at high speeds.

Far ahead, rapid flashes and much smoke indicated that furious attacks and counter-attacks were taking place between the rival destroyer flotillas and their supporting light cruisers. The battle area of these desperate conflicts between gun platforms of 1-inch steel, moving at the speed of an express train, was the space between the vans of the two Fleets.

We were too far off to see any details of this fighting; but at 6.47pm we reached the spot where it had taken place. The first thing we saw was a German three-funnel cruiser, the *Wiesbaden*. She was battered badly, as she had been lying inert between the two lines, and whenever a British battleship could not see her target she opened on the *Wiesbaden*.

We were simply longing to hit something, and this seemed our chance. Increasing speed to 20 knots we turned and led our squadron in to administer the *coup de grace*.

Turning to bring our broadsides to bear at 6,000 yards, we directed a stream of 6-inch on the Hun, who replied feebly with one gun. There is no doubt that the men who worked that gun had the right spirit in them.

Beyond the *Wiesbaden*, at a range of about 14,000 yards, our old friends the pre-Dreadnoughts were toddling along at the stern of the German line. During our approach to the *Wiesbaden* they had preserved an ominous silence. It did not remain thus for long. The six of them opened a rapid fire on us, and we were at once obliged to open the range without delay.

We scuttled back to the tail of the British line as hard as we could, zig-zagging like snipe with 11-inch crumping down ahead, on both sides, and astern of us.

I counted a bunch of three about 40 yards on the starboard beam of the ship, and H.B., who was hanging out over the other side of the after control, reported a group of seven close to the ship on the port beam. At this period (7.05pm) twilight was beginning, and the visibility was partly spoiled by low-lying clouds of funnel and brown cordite smoke, which hung like a gloomy pall over the scene.

It was apparent from the curve of our line that we were gradually working round to the eastward of the Huns, and at 7.30pm the Germans decided to make a supreme effort to get out of the nasty position they were being forced into, viz., the centre of a semi-circle, of which the British Fleet was the circumference.

That they got out very cleverly must be admitted. A few destroyers crept out at the head of their line, and almost immediately afterwards a dense smoke-screen unfurled itself between us and the enemy. Before this screen had reached its full length the Germans were altering course eight points together to starboard, and escaping from the deadly fire of the British battleships.

One of the minor incidents of battle now took place. A German destroyer, part of the debris of the destroyer actions some twenty minutes earlier, was lying, incapable of movement, between the two Fleets. Unfortunately for her, she was in such a position that the smoke-screen rolled to the southward of her. She was alone for her sins in front of the British Fleet.

No battleship fired at her; but we gave her a salvo at 6,000 yards as we came abreast of her. We hit, and a large explosion took place amidships. However, she still managed to float, and the *Faulkner* and some destroyers, who were hanging about near us, went over and finished her off. It rather annoyed us, as we intended to do some more target practice on her.

The Germans had disappeared somewhere to the south-west behind their smoke, and for a few minutes everything was strangely calm.

At 8.25pm the *Birmingham* sighted a submarine, and I saw that the Grand Fleet had got into five columns for the night. Four columns were abreast of each other, and the fifth, composed of the *Valiant*, *Malaya*, and *Barham*, was astern of them. We were on the starboard beam of the latter column. The course of the Fleet was south, and the Germans were somewhere to the westward of us in the growing darkness.

At 8.50pm we sighted four German destroyers approaching us on the starboard bow, apparently intending to deliver an attack on the Fifth Battle Squadron.

We opened fire at once, and hit the leading destroyer amidships. All four turned round and, pursued by our shells, disappeared behind a smoke-screen.

Curiously enough, I met the captain of this damaged destroyer, at a later period in the war, under different circumstances. For he left the German destroyer service soon after Jutland, and entered submarines. In the fullness of time his boat was destroyed, and he was the only survivor. Under my care he journeyed to London and a prison camp – but I am straying from Jutland.

This feeble little destroyer attack may be said to mark the conclusion of the day's action as far as we were concerned. Directly afterwards we went to night defence stations, and nerve-strings were tightened up another turn.

I busied myself in getting the notes I had taken into shape and testing communications to the guns. I have a curious little note on a crumpled signal pad. It is dated 8.50pm, and says: 'I see I've smoked five ounces of tobacco since half past three.'

II

At 9.00pm, heavy firing started, and the south-eastern horizon was lit by flashes. I subsequently discovered that this was the Third Light Cruiser Squadron and our battle cruisers still worrying and harassing the head of the German line and forcing them farther and farther away from their bases and out into the North Sea.

H.B. and I were fortunate enough to discover a slab of chocolate and some strong tea which refreshed us greatly. We were drinking about our tenth cup when some dark shapes appeared on the starboard bow, and in a couple of minutes resolved themselves into a flotilla of destroyers approaching on opposite courses and at a high speed. We held our fire, and when they were about 1,000 yards off recognised them as our own.

There had been no time to get the cumbersome challenge and recognition signal started. They flashed past us, and as the last one passed, her after-gun fired a solitary 4-inch shell in our direction. It whistled harmlessly overhead.

I account for this rude behaviour by supposing that at this gun some gun layer was dozing away, and happened to wake up as we were passing. Seeing the dim outlines of some light cruisers, he obeyed his first instinct and pressed the trigger. We quietly steamed on astern of the fleet; there was nothing to do except stare out to starboard and imagine vague shapes. It was very easy to imagine ships on the night of 31 May 1916.

At about 10.00pm, searchlights criss-crossed on the far western horizon; they rose and fell, turned and twisted, and finally fixed their implacable and relentless light on a group of destroyers.

Fascinated, we watched the destroyers rushing up the bright paths of the lights. The white splashes gleamed all round them, and then a great red lurid stain started in one of the attacking craft and spread to a vast explosion of fierce white flame, beside which the cruel searchlight seemed pale. Instantly the searchlights were extinguished, the attack was over, and once more all was dark.

We had probably witnessed one of the many and glorious attacks in which the British destroyer flotillas threw themselves without stint upon the German Fleet throughout this strange night.

The sudden disappearance of all signs of this attack ever having been made, left a curious feeling of emptiness in the atmosphere.

I groped my way on to the bridge and had a chat with B——, the gunnery lieutenant, as a result of which he arranged that in the event of night action he would control the guns from the fore-bridge and I would be in general charge aft.

A signalman, and R.I——, the navigator, suddenly whispered 'Five ships on the beam.'

The Commodore looked at them through night-glasses, and I heard a whispered discussion going on as to whether they were the enemy or the Third Light Cruiser Squadron.

From their faint silhouettes it was impossible to discover more than the fact that they were light cruisers. I decided to go aft as quickly as possible. On the way aft I looked in at the after control, where H.B. said to me, 'There are five Huns on the beam. What on earth is going on?'

They were evidently in as much doubt as us, for as I got down to the waist by the mainmast, a very great many things happened in a very short time.

We began to challenge; the Germans switched on coloured lights at their fore yardarms.

A second later a solitary gun crashed forth from the *Dublin*, who was next astern of us. Simultaneously I saw the shell hit a ship just above the waterline, and about 800 yards away.

As I caught a nightmare-like glimpse of her interior, which has remained photographed on my mind to this day, I said to myself, 'My G——, they are alongside us!'

At that moment the Germans switched on their searchlights, and we switched on ours. Before I was blinded by the lights in my eyes, I caught sight of a line of light grey ships. Then the gun behind which I was standing answered my shout of 'Fire!'

The action lasted 3½ minutes. The four leading German ships concentrated their lights and guns on the *Southampton*; the fifth and perhaps the fourth as well fired at the *Dublin*.

The *Nottingham* and *Birmingham*, third and fourth in our line, with great wisdom did not switch on their lights, and were not fired at.

In those 3½ minutes we had eighty-nine casualties, and 75 per cent. of the personnel on the upper deck were killed or wounded.

It is impossible to give a connected account of what happened. Many strange and unpleasant things happen when men find themselves in hell on earth. Men, strong men, go mad and jump overboard. Wounded men are driven to the oblivion of death in the sea by the agony of their injuries. It is not good to look too closely into these things which are the realities – the plain facts of battle.

The range was amazingly close – no two groups of such ships have ever fought so close in the history of this war. There could be no missing. A gun was fired and a hit obtained – the gun was loaded, it flamed, it roared, it leapt to the rear, it slid to the front – there was another hit.

But to load guns there must be men, flesh and blood must lift the shells and cordite and open and close the hungry breeches. But flesh and blood cannot stand high explosives, and there was a great deal of HE bursting all along HMS *Southampton*'s upper deck from her after screen to the fore bridge.

The range was so close, the German shots went high, just high enough to burst on the upper deck and around the after superstructure and bridge. And in a light cruiser that's where all the flesh and blood has to stand.

So in a very few seconds my guns stopped firing, all through lack of flesh and blood – it was a great pity. In fact, the sergeant-major, with his burnt face, and myself, seemed to be the only bits of flesh and blood left standing.

Where on earth were the others?

Why had the men on each side of me fallen down in such funny heaps? It was curious, very curious; as a matter of fact, daylight revealed that it wasn't so very remarkable. The really remarkable thing was that the sergeant-major, with his burnt face, and myself, were still standing about and representing flesh and blood.

One shell had burst on the side just below the gun, and the fragments had whipped over the top of the low bulwark and mowed the men down as standing corn falls before the reaper.

Another shell had burst on the searchlight just above us, and hurled the remains of this expensive instrument many feet. Three men who looked after it and had guided its beam on to the enemy died instantaneously.

The fragments from this shell descended upon 'the waist' like hail, and scoured out the insides of the gun-shields of the two 6-inch manned by marines, one gun each side. And then I seemed to be standing in a fire. The flash of some exploding shell had ignited half a dozen rounds of cordite.

A shell exploding in the half-deck had severed the connection to the upper deck fire main. I put my head down a hatch and shouted for a good hose. The wine steward came up on deck with one, someone turned on the water down below, and the fire was quickly out.

The wine steward forgot his servitude, he rose to the heights of an officer, he was my right-hand man. He spoke words of fierce exhortation to the wounded; those who could get up did so.

Then it became lighter than the day.

I looked forward.

Two pillars of white flames rose splendidly aloft. One roared up the foremast, the other reached above the tops of the second and third funnels.

This then was the end. The heat warmed the cheek. It was bad luck, just after we had got the small fire aft extinguished. But there could be no doubt; the central ammunition hoist was between those two funnels.

What was it going to feel like to blow up?

Let me see, how had the *Queen Mary* looked?

Of course, we were a smaller ship, perhaps we would blow up in a gentler manner.

Might as well take one's greatcoat off, just in case one fetched up in the water. I took it off.

What ought one to do?

Could not be more than a few seconds now. What could one do in a few seconds?

Could not fire a gun – no men.

Fascinating sight, those two pillars of white flame.

By Heaven, the centre one had turned red, it wavered, it decreased in height, it grew again; but the spell was broken, and I rushed to the ladder which led from the waist to the boat deck in order to get up to the fire and assist.

I ran a few steps and tripped up, over a heap of bodies. I got up, tried not to tread on soft things, and arrived on the boat deck.

The firing had ceased, the Commander and H.B. were at the central fire. It suddenly went out; so did the foremost one.

Everything was pitch black.

Where were the Germans?

Nothing but groans from dark corners.

Though I did not know it at the time, the Germans had fled.

They fled because A—— our torpedo lieutenant, had fired a 21-inch torpedo. At 41 knots the torpedo had shot across and, striking the *Frauenlob*, had blown her in half. Out of her 700 Huns, seven survived.

I have their account of the action before me.

They say: 'The leading ship of the British line burst into flame and blew up ... then we were torpedoed.' They were wrong, their friends sheered off just a few seconds too soon.

I will admit that they probably think they saw us blown up. A friend of mine, M'G———, who was 5 miles away in one of the Fifth Battle Squadron, read a signal on the bridge by the light of our fires.

In the ships of our squadron astern they thought we had gone, and took shelter from the bits they expected to come down.

It was a near thing.

It is after the firing is over that the real horror of a night action begins. We did not know where the Germans were, our guns' crews were practically non-existent, the voice-pipes and telephones to the guns were in shreds. We simply had to have time to reorganise, so we didn't dare show a light.

Yet the upper deck was strewn with dead and wounded. One stumbled on them as one walked. By the aid of discreetly struck matches and shaded torches the upper deck was searched.

I heard a groan and came upon a poor boy named M———. He could only say, 'My leg, my arm.' Another man and myself got him down one of the two steep hatches that led to the lower deck. His injuries were sickening, but with a smile he said, 'It's no good worrying about me, sir!' and then he died. I don't think he felt any pain.

I went up to the bridge to see B——— about reorganizing the men left for guns' crews and rigging up temporary communications. As I passed the chart house a well-known voice called me in. It was the Commodore.

He told me to go down to the fleet surgeon and find out what our casualties were. And once more I went below.

I went down the foremost hatch and along the central passage, nick-named the two-penny tube, which in this class of ship runs down the centre of the ship above the boiler and engine-rooms. There was about six inches of water in this passage, which had slopped in from some holes almost exactly on the water-lines.

The operating room, at the after end of this passage, was the stokers' bathroom.

Imagine a small room which a shore-goer might hesitate to use as a dark-room in his house, it might get so stuffy. The size of the room was about 8 feet high, 12 feet broad and 12 feet long. The centre of the room was occupied by a light portable operating table. A row of wash basins ran down one side, and the steel walls streamed with sweat.

Four bright electric lights were fixed to the roof, but with its faults the stokers' bathroom had some advantages. It had a tiled floor and a drain in the corner.

Stepping carefully between rows of shapes who were lying in lines down each side of the passage-way, I put my head inside the narrow doorway.

Bare-armed, the fleet surgeon and C——, the young doctor, were working with desperate but methodical haste. They were just taking a man's leg off above the knee, so I did not interrupt. When they were finished and the patient had been carried out, I gave the PMO the Commodore's message, whilst his assistants went outside to get another man.

'About forty killed and forty or fifty wounded,' he said.

I thanked him, and went back to the bridge.

He was hard at it for eleven hours; truly the doctor is one of the finest products of modern civilisation.

I told the Commodore what I had learned. He made a remark. I realised we were only one light cruiser in a very big fleet.

I went aft again and down to the ward-room. The mess presented an extraordinary appearance. As it was the largest room in the ship, we placed all the seriously wounded cases in it. The long table was covered with men, all lying very still and silently white.

The young doctor was in charge, and as I came in he signalled to the sick-berth steward to remove one man over whom he had been bending. Four stokers, still grimy from the stoke-hole, lifted the body and carried it out.

Two men were on top of the sideboard, others were in armchairs.

A hole in the side admitted water to the ward-room, which sploshed about as the ship gently rolled. In this ankle-deep flood, bloodstained bandages and countless pieces of the small debris of war floated to-and-fro.

All the wounded who could speak were very cheerful and only wanted one thing – cigarettes. The most dreadful cases were the 'burns' – this subject cannot be written about.

An hour's work on deck connected with the reorganisation of the guns' crews, the impressment of stokers off watch for this duty, and the testing of communications followed. Then H.B. and myself, we'd sit down somewhere. We went up to the fore-bridge, and rolled ourselves up in the canvas cover of a compass.

Horrors! it was wet. We hastily shifted to a less gruesome bed.

We had just lain down when fresh gun-firing broke out right astern, and everyone was on the *qui vive* with a jump. It died down – I wasn't sorry, we were not as ready for action as we could have wished.

We increased speed to 20 knots, and as dawn slowly grew the ghostly shapes of some battleships loomed out of the mist. I heard a pessimist on the upper bridge hazard the opinion that we were about to take station astern of the German Battle Fleet, but as the light grew brighter we saw that we had rejoined the British Fleet.

Complete daylight enabled us to survey the damage. The funnels were riddled through with hundreds of small holes, and the decks were slashed and ripped with splinters. There were several holes along the side, but the general effect was as if handfuls of splinters had been thrown against the upper works of the ship. The protective mattresses round the bridge and control position were slashed with splinters. The fore-mast, the rigging, the boats, the signal lockets, the funnel casing, the main mast, everything was a mass of splinter holes.

Our sailors firmly believed, and continued to do so up to the day on which I left the ship, that we had been deluged with shrapnel. It was certainly surprising that any one on the upper deck remained un-hit.

The flag lieutenant, one P—— by name, had a remarkable escape. The secretary asked him what he had done to his cap during the night. P—— took it off, and there was a large rent where a splinter, which must have been shaped something like a skewer, had entered his cap just above his ear and out again through the crown. P—— had felt nothing. This sounds almost impossible, but I can vouch for its absolute truth.

There were other curious escapes.

O——, the paymaster, was sitting in the decoding office under the waist when the action began. A shell came through the side, passed through the canvas walls of the decoding office and burst near the ward-room, taking a man's head off en route. O—— 'felt a wind!'

H.B. was leaning over the ledge of the after control when a shell passed through a bracket supporting the ledge he was leaning over. From here it went through the funnel and burst with deadly effect in the inside of a gun shield of one of the guns on the disengaged side.

The Commodore walked round the upper deck at about 9 o'clock, and was loudly cheered.

The morale of the crew was splendid.

It suddenly occurred to me that I might as well go and have a look at my cabin. I got through the watertight doors and discovered an extra-ordinary scene of confusion in the foremost cabin flat. Three shells had burst therein, and one had apparently chosen my cabin for its final effort. The place was smashed to pieces, and water was smashing in through a small hole in the ship's side.

I've only seen one sight comparable to it, and that was the inside of a German submarine after a strong party of souvenir hunters had been invited to go round her.

I paddled about, feeling like a lost soul, for a few moments, in what had been rather a fashionable cabin, and then retired, closing the watertight door on the beastly scene.

My first impulse, which I obeyed, was to find S. B—— and one or two others and invite them to look at their cabins – even thus can joy be extracted from the sorrows of others.

To return to the movements of the ship.

As soon as it was daylight, squadrons had sorted themselves out, and we searched about until we discovered the *Lion* and other battle cruisers, to whom we attached ourselves.

A Zepp passed overhead at 10.00am, but otherwise we saw no signs of the enemy, though we cruised about in different directions.

At noon it became evident that the Huns had got in, and so the signal was made for the Fleet to return to its bases.

Soon after lunch on our way north we passed the bow of a destroyer sticking up out of the water, and nearby we steamed through an immense oily and smooth pool of water, which doubtless marked the resting place of some great ship.

In the afternoon the Commodore held a short service in the waist. It was a moving scene. Overhead the main-top mast, which had been half shot through, swayed giddily about and seemed likely to go over the side or come down on the boat deck at any moment. In serried lines the officers and men stood bare-headed round the Commodore, who read a few of the wonderful prayers for the use of those at sea. I think we all felt strangely moved.

That night the weather became nasty, and we had trouble with the temporary shores and plugs that had been improvised for the holes near the waterline, We had to heave to for short periods. I spent most of the night either on the bridge or searching for a sleeping billet.

Next day we continued on our course for Rosyth, which place we reached at 2.00am. We were the last ship of the Battle Cruiser Force to enter harbour, and as the battle cruisers had been in since 2.00am our belated appearance caused much relief amongst certain ladies ashore.

On our way in we had buried a poor fellow who had lain like a marble statue on the ward-room table for thirty-six hours. There were no injuries upon him – he died of shock. I used to go in and look at him; he seemed so peaceful and still that it was almost impossible to believe that in that body life was yielding inch by inch to death.

The burial service at sea is the most poignant of all ceremonies. Doubtless he had welcomed the sight of May Island many times as we returned from trips in the North Sea, and as his body slid from beneath the Union Jack into the waters bubbling along our side there was a silence in which as if by a pre-arranged signal the voice of the lookout floated aft: 'Land on the port bow.' It was May Island.

As soon as we had anchored, hospital drifters came alongside, and the wounded were lifted out in cots and transferred to an adjacent hospital ship.

It was this afternoon that a reaction began to set in. Everyone was very snappy and irritable, there were horrible rumours (with a basis of truth, I regret to say) that men landing from ships like the *Warspite*, that had been in some time, had been the object of hostile demonstrations ashore.

It was impossible to find out any facts as to what damage the Germans had sustained; and our own losses had been only too apparent. There were depressing gaps in the line of battle cruisers where the three lost ships had been in the habit of lying.

I felt very miserable, largely due, I think, to lack of sleep, and to the fact that the ward-room being uninhabitable, and my cabin wrecked, I had nowhere to go to. There was also the official Communiqué – a bit of a damper. I felt I wanted to burst into tears, hit somebody, or do something equally foolish.

At 5.00pm a definite order to go into the basin of Rosyth Dockyard relieved the strain, and, with a job in hand, every one became cheery again. As we were slowly wharfed through the lock gates, large crowds assembled to greet us, chiefly composed of dockyard men, and men from the *Warspite*, and survivors of the *Warrior*, which had sunk some 80 miles from the action, after being towed by the *Engadine*.

The survivors of the *Warrior* were garbed in a mixture of uniform and plain clothes, and were in great spirits. They were making much of the men of the *Warspite*, to which ship they rightly ascribed their salvation, as had the *Warspite* not turned in towards the German line when she did, there is little doubt the *Warrior* would have followed the *Defence* in a very short space of time.

Next day most of the officers and crew went on leave, a few men under my command being left to superintend the refit.

The Commodore shifted his broad pennant to the *Birmingham* whilst we were out of action.

Before our ship's company went on leave Sir David Beatty came on board and made us a very charming and complimentary speech.

During the three weeks in which we were being repaired at Rosyth, we had a great many visitors on board, including His Majesty the King, to whom I had the honour of being presented.

The Prime Minister (Mr Asquith) and a party also visited the ship. I was showing him my cabin, and he commented on the damage to my private effects. I was about to strike when the iron was hot, and hit at the desirability of bringing pressure to bear on the Treasury to treat all claims in a broad-minded manner, when I suddenly recollected that, as my guest was First Lord of the Treasury, he might think it somewhat pointed if I enlarged on the iniquities of that department.

Large parties of technical sightseers came up from the Admiralty, the gunnery school (Whaley), and the torpedo school (*Vernon*), and swarmed over the ship, asking innumerable questions and taking notes.

The *Tiger*, *Princess Royal*, and *Warspite* were in dock alongside us, and I had a good look at all their damage, and heard many interesting stories of their share in the action.

On 17 June I went on leave, and was more than glad to see dear old London again. When I returned, in a penniless condition, on 29 June, we were once more back in our old billet off Charlestown, and flagship of the Second Light Cruiser Squadron.

In one way we were changed. There were sixty new faces amongst the ship's company, and as these new arrivals had joined no ordinary ship, but a ship with a reputation, we started as hard as we could to train them up in the way they should go.

CHAPTER FIVE

'Q' SHIP *RESULT*

By G.H.P. Mulhauser

Lieutenant M—— had seen service with the Harwich destroyers and at Gallipoli, and had taken part in the landings. He was subsequently invalided out of the service. On leaving hospital he was taken on to the Emergency List, and appointed to the command of the armed yacht *Lady Blanche* at Milford Haven. While there he contracted pleurisy as the result of exposure, and had to go to hospital again. When cured he was appointed to the Lowestoft Base for 'Light shore duty,' and managed to persuade the authorities that the command of a sailing 'Q' ship came properly under that heading.

I never regretted my decision to join the schooner. As far as food and personal comfort were concerned, she was no better than the smacks, if anything rather worse, but she was a 'happy' ship, and there seemed a good chance of doing useful work in her. We all had the greatest confidence in our CO, and felt that he would make the most of any chance that occurred.

As armament she carried two 18cwt 12-pounder guns, one forward and one aft of the mainmast, in gun-wells sunk into what had been the cargo hatches. They were very inconspicuous, and ships have come right alongside and not noticed them. The bulwarks opposite to them on each side were cut, and could be lowered when in action. In addition she had a pounder gun on the port side for'd, and two fixed 14 inch torpedo tubes aft, one on each quarter. These pointed astern at an angle of 30 degrees to the line of the keel. The galley was on deck just abaft the foremast. The RNR (T) ratings, mostly fishermen, lived in the fo'c'sle, and a mess deck for the active service ratings was put up in what had been the for'd hold. An alleyway led from the mess deck to the magazine amidships, and continued through it to a ladder giving access to the deck. Lieutenant M—— and I had a cabin aft of the magazine on the starboard side of this alleyway, and on the opposite side were the W/T cabin, and another used at first by the sailing master, J. Reid, and later turned into a storeroom. In M——'s half of the cabin were a bunk, seat, table, lamp, looking-glass, and washing basin, while my half was similarly fitted, except that there was no washing basin. A stove stood in the middle, and was supposed to divide it into two cabins.

Aft of the mizzenmast was a companionway leading to the engine room, and to a very small cabin where we took our meals. The engine was a hot bulb paraffin motor giving a speed of about 3 knots, just enough to manoeuvre with when in action. A small Douglas engine on deck supplied the motive power to the W/T dynamo, and the triatic stay was turned into an aerial. We could send messages about 40 miles, and could, of course, receive them from much greater distances.

Steel air bottles were also fitted containing air compressed to about 1,800lbs. to the square inch for 'topping up' the compressed air in the torpedoes,

By way of ballast 100 tons of sand were taken on board. This was not ideal ballast, as it meant that the ship had no reserve buoyancy, and would start to sink should the hull be pierced by a shell.

A small boat, capable of taking nine men, was carried in davits over the counter.

For variety and disguise we went out sometimes as a topsail schooner, i.e., with yards and square topsails on the foremast, and sometimes with fore and aft topsails only. The sails were also changed from time to time, and were white on some trips and tanned on others, or half and half. Stringent rules were also made as to the number of men who might appear on deck at one time, as the ordinary coasting schooner of our size would only carry about five men, and we had to conform to the habits of coasting vessels in every respect. Of course no one appeared in uniform, and all wore what they liked, and the older the clothes were the better. Lieutenant M——— had a great idea that the proper headgear for a coasting skipper was a hard felt hat, and he appeared in one which would have graced Bond Street. He was very reluctant to give it up, and before doing so knocked a hole in the top to allow his hair to appear through the opening, hoping in this way to make it more convincing and to discount its stylish shape. But he had to give it up in the end. The men took to wearing hard hats, and he felt that he could not compete.

Altogether there were twenty-three men on board, of whom eleven were active service ratings, and the rest RNR (T), mostly fishermen, with a few from the coasting trade. They were all volunteers, and were a good crowd. Only volunteers were taken in these 'Q' ships. The notice asking for volunteers stated that the work was 'hazardous, at times monotonous, and not free from discomfort.' The last clause was correct at any rate. Extra pay was offered, which the men called 'danger' money, but which was really extra 'hard lying' money. This allowance is usually given to those serving in small ships, which are crowded and very uncomfortable, especially in bad weather. It varied with the class of ship, submarines and 'Q' ships getting the highest rate.

Fitting out, which, by the way, was done alongside an open quay so that everyone in Lowestoft knew about us, was a long affair, and it was not before 3 February 1917, that we were ready for some of the trials, and incidentally were hotly chased by a patrol, who evidently thought that it was unseemly for a coaster suddenly to start firing guns. He belonged to Yarmouth or he would have known who we were.

Four days later we ran the torpedoes. One would not start, and the other would not stop, but ran for 3 miles at a slow speed. We captured it in the end. The trouble was found to be caused by ice in the works.

On 9 February we left for our first trip. I was full of high hopes, and expected to have a share in great doings. I placed a lot of confidence in the torpedoes, which they were far from deserving. M—— said nothing to damp my enthusiasm, and appeared outwardly to share my hopes, but he had been in action several times and had had a good deal of experience, and no doubt had his own opinion on the subject. I doubt whether he really expected to see the fulfilment of the vision of enemy light cruisers – TBDs were too paltry – mortally wounded by our deadly 'mouldies', and sinking. I doubt whether I really believed that myself.

It did not take us long to realise how true had been the description that the job was not free from discomfort. Though rather crowded the men were not quite as badly off as we were, as our little cabin aft where we had our meals was always full of acrid fumes from the blow-lamp in the engine room. This blowlamp had to be kept going continually to keep the bulb hot, and emitted a constant roar, and at times the most noxious fumes. Otherwise we were not so badly off except that the cabins leaked like sieves, and the cooking was poor.

The handling of the ship gave no trouble. The fishermen were all used to sails, and there were quite a large proportion of the active service ratings who had been sailing in ships in the Persian Gulf. In addition there were J. Reid, the sailing master, and Palmer, the mate, both of whom were schooner men. The latter of these went into hospital at the end of the first trip suffering from chill, and J. Reid left soon afterwards to go to a trawler. Ultimately we abolished these two positions, and put the petty officer and the two leading seamen in charge of a watch each, while the CO and I worked watch and watch, one of us being always about. One small alteration had to be made at the end of the first trip. The point at which the ship pivoted was too far aft, and she would not 'stay', or in other words come round when close hauled. This fault was cured by moving some of the ballast further forward.

In light winds she was slow, but got along fairly well in strong breezes.

Nothing much happened on the first trip. The next time we went out in a dense fog. The people at the Base thought that fog was what we wanted when at sea. 'A submarine might run into you,' they said. There certainly was a chance that something might run into us, but it was not likely to be a submarine. However, no doubt they knew best, and we went. Off the Shipwash Light Ship a bunch of destroyers missed us by a few feet, but after that we got clear of the traffic, and made for the North Hinder Lightship. While we were wending our way slowly northwards one of the torpedo ratings, an AB, accidentally fired off one of the torpedoes. It leapt out of its tube, crashed against the bulwark, burst open the port, and disappeared in a cloud of smoke. The AB danced on the deck, and waved his arms in despair. It is a serious thing to lose a torpedo, and later on in port, a Court of Enquiry sat to consider the matter. All who were on deck at the time appeared as witnesses. The CO went in first, while we waited outside. He was asked what steps he had taken to recover the torpedo, and how often the men were drilled at the torpedoes. He replied that being on special service he had not taken any steps to recover it, and for the same reason never had any torpedo drill, and that, moreover, his torpedo ratings were trained men, and drill was not necessary. These reasons were held to be sound. The AB was then sent for. 'Now tell us,' they said to him, 'how often do you have torpedo drill in your ship?' 'Every day, sir,' stoutly replied the AB. The Court smiled grimly. The AB left feeling that he had done his duty and supported his Officers, and the LTO was actuated by similar ideas when he came to the CO on our return to port and asked him what reply he was to make if questioned about the missing torpedo. He was quite prepared to swear that it had been fired at a Fritz, or make any statement indicated and in so doing would have felt that he was doing the right thing. Any other course, such as telling the truth, would have seemed to him dishonourable.

It was while on this trip that we were encouraged by sighting a periscope. There had been a dense fog all the morning, but in the afternoon it cleared slightly, and it was possible to see for a mile all round. One of the hands suddenly sighted a periscope on the starboard bow. The alarm was given, and the men crawled to action stations. The periscope appeared again on the beam, and then astern, finally coming up on the port quarter. I cannot say that I saw it myself, but several of the hands made it out. We waited for developments, which might be expected to take the form of a torpedo, but nothing came, and the engineman, Macalpine, found that he had put on his silk blouse and toque for no purpose. His position in action station was at the head of the engine room companion-way, clad, as to the upper part of his body, in feminine attire. We hoped that Fritz would conclude that the skipper's wife was on board, and, being by nature a boastful animal, would come alongside to play the heavy conqueror. With the same idea a skirt, a blouse, stockings, and bloomers hung on a line stretched between the main and mizzen shrouds. We pinned great faith in these as a guarantee of our peaceful character. On this occasion, however, Fritz remained coy, and after hovering about submerged for an hour, went off.

At the beginning of March we were sent out to make a tour round by the North Hinder Lightship, up past Smith's Knoll and then to the Dogger Bank. 'Don't be away too long,' the SNO had told M——, 'I am always very anxious when you are out.' M—— was pleased at this evidence of interest in the part of the SNO, and told Captain B——, the second in command at the Base, about it. The Captain laughed heartily, and said: 'That's good. Why, last time you were entering the harbour I went to him and told him the *Result* was coming in, and he said: 'Coming in? I did not know that she was out!' Apparently his anxiety was not very acute after all, as it had not even caused him to take the trouble to find out whether we were safe in harbour or at sea.

The first three days out were quiet, but on the morning of the fourth day it began to breeze up, and in the early hours the flying jib had to be taken in. An hour later the outer jib was stowed, and the mizzen, main, and foresails reefed. At dark a heavy SE gale was blowing, and things were very uncomfortable. The CO decided to heave to, as the ship was then clear of minefields, and also clear of the SW Patch on the Dogger Bank.

The inner jib was stowed, staysail hauled to windward, another reef taken in the mizzen, and mainsails, and the foresail lowered. The latter made a gallant fight of it, and it took two watches to subdue it. The helm was then put down, and she came up to the wind. The sea was by this time very high, the heaviest I had yet seen in the North Sea, and she rolled, and wallowed. She was perfectly safe, but very uncomfortable. The worst feature was the way the decks leaked. This was not, of course, the fault of the ship, but arose from bad shipwright work, but it made things very uncomfortable. Water poured in streams into our cabins, and into the storerooms and magazine under the gun-well. Reid abandoned his cabin and went and established himself aft. All our clothes were wet, and we had to do our turn on deck wet to the skin. Every four hours the ship was pumped out, a job which took about half an hour each time. Meals became dreadful affairs. Cooking was out of the question, but tea was made, and we managed with that, and tinned meat. Our marine servant was ill, but one of the deckhands, Ward, looked after us and brought the tea. His round, cheerful face appearing in the doorway was quite a tonic. The meals themselves were great scrambles. The table cloth was filthy with spilt tea and tea leaves and scraps from the plates, and everything seemed to have been in contact with either the butter or the marmalade. Things had reached such a state of chaos below that it became rather amusing, but the watches on deck were not so pleasant. There was not much to do there seeing that nothing had carried away. The first few minutes usually sufficed for water to get into one's boots, and after that nothing much mattered. It was only a question of endurance then, and of dodging the waves which leaped playfully over the rail from time to time. A fine, big fellow crashed on to Capps, one of the deckhands, as he made his way forward. He disappeared from view. Someone shouted out that he had been knocked down, but I could see his yellow oilskin, and knew that he would come into sight again shortly. The water cleared away , and there he was clinging to the shrouds. He seemed to look on the affair as a joke against himself, and turned to see if we had noticed the incident. He was amused, and went forward chuckling to himself.

In the afternoon a fine steam trawler came rolling towards us. She was on patrol, and having sighted us came up for a closer inspection. We hoisted a signal: 'What is my present position?' According to calculations we had been making 2 miles of leeway, and a half-mile of headway in the hour since we had been hove to, but the CO thought that it would be as well to verify the estimated position. The trawler, the *Lordship*, replied: '55° north latitude, 56° east longitude,' and on our making 'Thank you,' hoisted 'I wish you a pleasant voyage.' Perhaps the skipper was indulging in a little playful sarcasm. I expect that his signalman laughed as he looked out and hoisted the flags. The position given was 15 miles NE of our estimated position, a difference which was not surprising considering that we had not been able to get any sights for the two previous days, while our speed, leeway, set, and strength of the tides had to be estimated.

We had then been hove to for nearly 24 hours, and the barometer was still going down, and the weather getting worse. The CO decided to run for shelter. But where could we go? The air was thick with driving spray blown off the tops of the waves, and, moreover, no shore navigating lights were exhibited. It would therefore be madness to run for any of the ports on the coast, as that would be running for a lee shore, which would be invisible when we reached it. We wanted somewhere with a wide entrance, and the Firth of Forth 140 miles away to the north-west was the only place that we could safely make for. At 5.00pm, therefore, sheets were slacked off, and the helm put up. She soon paid off and gathered way, and staggered along at 8 knots in a series of wild lurches. Seas caught her under the counter, and sent her reeling off her course, and the helmsman had a busy time. Seas with breaking tops climbed on board most of the time and in the evening a real big fellow arrived. For some reason I looked round whilst standing aft near the helmsman, and saw a wave close to the starboard counter, and just about to break. It towered above me, and came bodily on board, beating me to my knees. Volumes of water poured into the engine room, and wild Scotch (*sic.*) curses from Macalpine, and steam poured out. Soon after midnight the ship was gybed, and a course set for the Longstone Lighthouse. This alteration made mine a lee bunk, and a stream of water on to my face called my attention to the fact. Water was coming down the ventilator, and the hatch was also making a generous contribution. I turned out, rescued my clogs, which were floating about, and waded along the alleyway to the mess-deck. Things there were in a state of great confusion, and the place was full of wet clothes hanging on lines. One watch was just coming down, and I sent one man aft to screw down the ventilator. I then turned in again for the balance of the watch. The CO remained on deck all through the middle watch, in case we were rather further west than we thought, in which case we were likely to go ashore about that time. At 4.00am that danger still existed, and I warned the look-outs to keep their eyes open. At 9.00am the Longstone Lighthouse was sighted well to port, so our course had been about right after all. We had still a long way to go, and if we were to get in before dark something must be done to increase the speed. The CO decided to set the lower topsail. This steadied her very much, and sensibly increased our pace. At 3.00pm May Island was due. We were very anxious to sight it ahead, so that we could pass it on the north side, as the south side had been mined by enemy submarines. But at 3.00pm nothing could be seen through the driving mist. Half an hour later, however, land appeared on the starboard beam, May Island at last, but on the wrong side! It was too late to do anything in the way of altering course. If the mines were still there, we were among them, and must take our chance. Only the CO and I knew that there was any danger. We passed safely through. By 7.00pm we were through the boom, and had anchored in Aberlady Bay. It was an immense relief to get in, and to take off our wet clothes, and have a rough bath by a warm fire.

They told us at Granton, when we got there, that the gale had been a very severe one, and had done a lot of damage on shore.

After a few days spent in making good some defects we sailed again on 12 March. Two days later the alarm gong sounded. A submarine had come to the surface 1½ miles away. It was, however, a British submarine returning from patrol, but next day we came across a Fritz, and had our baptism of fire. The wind was freshening at the time, and we were just lowering and stowing the topsails when a submarine was sighted coming up astern, and immediately afterwards the report of a gun was heard. In a few seconds the men were at their stations, but only five showed on deck. The CO ordered the helm to be put down, to bring the ship into the wind, and the headsails to be hauled down. While this was happening shells were dropping around and bursting. One of them grazed the flying jib stay, and went on making a most curious whistling noise. The submarine commander refused to accept our apparent surrender, and continued firing steadily from a distance of 2,000 yards. The CO then ordered the panic party to abandon ship. The men in 'Q' ships who were told off to abandon ship when in action were termed the 'panic party'. They were practised in showing the proper amount of scare. On this occasion they made a gallant attempt to capsize the boat when lowering it. We thought that this would give a realistic touch to the affair, but the boat refused to capsize and righted itself when it reached the water, and they had to get into it as it was. Reid and four hands were then in the boat, and they were supposed to represent the whole of the crew, while the ship was lying head to wind with the sails flapping, and apparently deserted. No one showed on deck, but below the bulwarks were the three guns' crews lying alongside their guns, the LTO alongside his torpedo tubes, the engineers standing by the motor ready to start it when required, while the CO perambulated the deck on his hands and knees watching the course of events through holes in the bulwarks, and I sat on deck at the wheel trying to keep the ship in the wind so as not to get too far away from the boat. As soon as the latter left the ship the submarine ventured to approach to 1,000 yards, but would not come any closer. They went on firing from that distance for some time without hitting the hull or a spar. The sails and gear were cut about by shells and splinters, but as long as nothing vital was hit we could continue to lie low in the hope that it would come nearer. But that was just what it had not the slightest intention of doing unless it could first get hold of the boat. That, on the other hand, we could not allow, as with the boat alongside them we should not be able to fire should an opportunity occur. Things therefore remained at a sort of deadlock.

Reid rowed about first in one direction and then in another, as if he did not know what to do for the best, but he took care to keep within 200 yards of the ship. He said afterwards that he felt very lonely with a large and hostile submarine in his immediate neighbourhood, and the ship tending to work away from him. Never had the latter seemed to him so desirable. He even found time to admire the beauty of her lines. Then the submarine turned its gun on the boat, possibly with the idea of inducing it to approach, but it had the opposite result, and Reid rowed away. After firing three shells, the first of which went short, the second over, while the third nearly hit it, the submarine commander seemed to come to the conclusion that the men in the boat were too much upset to understand what was required, turned his attention to the ship once more. Our ordeal had started again. The CO on hands and knees, with his eye to a hole in the bulwarks, watched the firing in an impersonal and critical spirit. He considered that it was bad. The submarine was only 1,000 yards distant, and, though there was a nasty short sea which caused it to roll a good deal, he thought that it should have done better. It was firing about one shell short to about three over. 'Ah,' he said once, 'that was better, that very nearly hit the counter.' As I was sitting at the counter, it did not strike me at all as an admirable effort on their part. On the contrary; while added to the feeling of personal insecurity caused by shells and fragments of shells hurtling past one's ears, was a distinct feeling of humiliation. It was true that that was what we were there for, and it was all part of the game, but somehow it did not seem right to be sitting in water at an idle wheel, doing nothing, while a submarine plugged shells at the ship for what seemed an interminable time.

At length after the firing had gone on for 45 minutes, and the submarine commander seemed as determined as ever not to come any nearer, the CO decided to try and wing him as he was within easy range, and accordingly gave the word to open fire. The White Ensign shot aloft, the engine was started, down crashed the bulwarks, and round came the guns. The submarine had taken alarm at the first movement, and was doing a crash dive, but the aft 12-pounder, Gun-layer W. Wreford, AB, hit him at the base of the conning tower at its junction with the deck, and the 6-pounder, Gun-layer H.G. Wells, AB, also hit the conning tower higher up. The second shot from the 12-pounder missed. In 30 seconds the submarine had disappeared. Had we sunk it? We knew that the 12-pounder had hit it, and that in a good spot, but beyond that it was almost impossible to say anything. If it were still in fighting trim, it would almost certainly try and torpedo us, but though it had plenty of opportunities of so doing while we were picking up the boat, and though we sailed up to the spot where it had disappeared, we saw no more of it, and the conviction grew that it must have been destroyed, or at least badly damaged, or it would not have taken things lying down. After searching the area, and finding nothing, we resumed our course. Whether we had sunk it or not, we had at least given it a lesson in gunnery. Unmolested and firing at its ease it had failed to score a decisive hit in three quarters of an hour, while our first two shots had both hit, in spite of the fact that the guns had to be trained round from a fore and aft position to one on the beam. The for'd 12-pounder had not fired. It could not be brought to bear in time.

As the wind was increasing, and looked like getting worse, the CO decided to make for the coast, so as not to have a minefield under the lee in case of a gale. As soon as the ship was on the new course a submarine appeared ahead. At first we thought that it was our late opponent come to life again, and the ship was headed straight at it. But, as we were to discover shortly, it was not the same submarine but another one, and our alteration of course had evidently greatly puzzled the commander. When less than half a mile away he fired a torpedo to clear the air. It missed. He then opened fire. At the first report it was clear that we had to do with a fresh submarine, the note of the gun being quite different, but we had by then committed ourselves, and it was too late to think of abandoning ship, or acting the part of an innocent coaster, and word was passed to open fire. The first two rounds both missed fire (*sic.*), and by the time the cartridges had been extracted the submarine was diving, and almost out of sight. However, the gun-layer did get off one round, a snap shot which missed. There was then no reason to wait about, as the submarine would not come up again, and the ship was kept on her course.

And so ended our first scrap with a submarine, the battle of the South West Patch as we called it from the name of a neighbouring sandbank.

The sails and ropes were a good deal cut about – there were thirteen holes in the foresail alone – and we sailed down the coast in the direction of our port to refit. As Smith's Knoll was not much out of the way, the CO decided to have a look round there to see if anything was on foot. When nearing it at 11.00pm the alarm gong sounded. The CO started from sleep under the impression that someone was testing the circuits, but quickly realising that this would not be done at that hour he rushed on deck, and found a scene of some confusion. The night was dark, and a fresh breeze was blowing. The guns' crews worked feverishly to clear away their guns, and to add to the difficulties of the position, the helmsman accidentally gybed. As a result the three booms dashed noisily to and fro and further complicated matters.

'Where is the submarine?'

'On the port beam, sir,' replied the officer in charge of the deck in a hoarse whisper, anxious not to alarm the game. Then, the seaman coming suddenly uppermost, he shouted an order to the helmsman in a loud voice. No submarine, however, was to be seen on the port beam, or anywhere else, and it was, of course, hopeless to chase with a sailing ship in the dark. The two look-outs were cross-examined as to what they had seen.

'A black object close aboard about the size of a conning tower.'

'Was it under way?'

'No, sir, it seemed stopped.'

A black object, about the size of a conning tower, stopped. It sounded as if it might be a buoy, and on running out roughly the estimated position, it was seen that we were due to pass a black buoy about that time. This seemed to settle it, but to make quite sure the ship was hove to and the hydrophone lowered over the side. It gave the usual water noises, but no sound of a propeller. It must have been the buoy, and the men were dismissed, and the watch below turned in again.

Two days later we were in port having the damage made good.

For his share in the scrap Lieutenant M—— was mentioned in despatches, as was also J. Reid, who went away in the boat, and a letter from the Admiralty expressing the approval of My Lords of the behaviour of the ship's company was also received at the Base.

Some months later a very accurate account of the scrap, written presumably by the commander of the submarine, fell into the hands of the authorities, and the inference is that either *UC 45* (the number of the submarine) got home or that the crew did, possibly on board the second one.

On the next trip there was more excitement. We first made our way to the scene of the last encounter, but drew blank. A heavy gale then forced us to take shelter in the Wash. On coming out we made our way to Smith's Knoll, without seeing anything. At 4.00am on 5 April 1917, we had passed it, and were on our way to the North Hinder Lightship. It was rather thick, and the wind was very light. I had had my usual two cups of tea and was feeling very pleased with life in general, and especially with the prospect of a whole night in my bunk, when war's rude alarms were suddenly forced on my notice. A large submarine, which looked in the mist as big as a TBD, appeared ahead, and then as rapidly disappeared. The alarm was given, and there was a bustle for a few minutes, and then quiet. Everyone was at his post. The CO came on deck, as imperturbable as ever. He sauntered up to me in a casual sort of way to persuade the submarine, should it be watching through its periscope that it had not been sighted. With the same object the cook went to the galley and started preparing breakfast, while two of the hands scrubbed down. Just then a small upended spar was seen 100 yards on the port bow. It showed 2 feet clear of the water, and from the top a slight rod projected for another 4 feet and terminated in a square lump 6 inches in diameter. The lower portion might be a periscope, but what was the upper part? As we looked, it slowly dipped, and disappeared. It evidently was a periscope. A few minutes later it rose on the beam, but that time without the upper part, dipped after a short interval, showed on the quarter, astern, and on the starboard side. At each appearance it showed for about a minute, and then sank out of sight. This behaviour was rather disconcerting. To be closely examined in that indecent way through a sinister-looking periscope was as trying as being looked at through binoculars from a distance of 50 yards. After the submarine had examined us at its leisure from all points of view there was a pause of nearly half an hour. What was to be the next move? Had it gone off altogether, or was it working into position to torpedo us, which it could have done quite easily, or was it working away under water to a distance with the idea of coming to the surface a few miles off and shelling the ship? The CO thought that it was doing the latter, and that all we could do was to wait. The motor was started for manoeuvring purposes, and then we sat still, and thought of many things. To reduce the number of men showing, Reid took the wheel, the CO represented the skipper, two hands worked about the decks, and the cook went on with the breakfast. I sat in the engine-room hatchway out of sight with a notebook ready to record events. Suddenly a shell burst alongside followed by others, but no submarine was to be seen, and the CO could not make out from which direction they came, until he caught sight of a flash under the sun. In that position the submarine was quite invisible, while the ship made a perfect target with the sun full on her sails, and white hull. This submarine seemed to be a much more business-like fellow than the others we met on the last occasion. For one thing it had a bigger gun, 4.1-inch semi-automatic high velocity with an effective range of 13,500 yards. The shells arrived at terrific speed, and burst with an extremely vicious sound. It was firing fast and accurately, and after the first two or three shots was well on the target. The 'panic party' was ordered away, but before they could get clear a shell struck the ship amidships right on the waterline, penetrated the hull and burst inside, reducing the W/T cabin and the store-room to matchwood, and wrecking and setting fire to the magazine. There were two men of the ammunition party in there at the time, and one of them, Morris, was hurled right down the alleyway on to the stove in our cabin, and injured his back, while the other, Ryder, had the upper bone of his arm shattered and smashed to splinters, and was also wounded in the back. The next shell burst just short and flung sheets of water over the ship, wetting everyone to the skin at the same moment. A universal gasp went up. The water was very cold. The position was not very satisfactory. The ship had no reserve buoyancy, and the water pouring in through the hole in the side was already beginning to affect her. Reid, still at the wheel, found her slow to answer the helm and stated in a doleful voice: 'She is sinking, sir.' Dense clouds of smoke were pouring out of the hatches leading to the magazine. Some action seemed called for. It was not the slightest use sitting with folded hands, waiting either to sink or blow up, whichever should happen first. We might as well have a run for our money, and the CO gave the order to open fire. The gun-layers could not see the submarine hidden as it was in the mist under the sun, but they put 6,000 yards on the elevating dial, and fired over open sights at the horizon in the direction the submarine was supposed to be. Each gun fired two rounds and then stopped, as the submarine had not replied. It ceased firing immediately we opened up. There is no reason to suppose that any of our shells hit it, or even went near it. Submarines never fought it out on the surface as long as they could dive and escape in that way, and this one very likely started to dive as soon as he saw the flash of the first round without waiting for the shells to arrive. Its next step would probably be to come closer and torpedo us, but that we could not help, and in the meantime we had a few minutes to attend to the wounded, try and plug the hole in the side, and tackle the fire. The CO bandaged Ryder, who had been pulled out of the magazine and who lay motionless on deck, so still that I thought he was dead, while I set two hands to try and stop the leak with a couple of coal bags and a wooden shot hole plug. One of them went over the side and adjusted the bags and the plug, while the other hammered it home with the back of a long handled axe. I then went to see about the fire, as I expected that she would blow up if nothing was done. The place was full of smoke and fumes, and it was impossible to see anything. After stumbling about among the debris I found smouldering rockets and other things, but no active fire, and then returned to the deck, as the submarine was reported to have turned up again. It kept dead astern and watched through its periscope. If we had had more speed we might have been able to turn sufficiently to bring one of the torpedoes to bear. It would not run deep enough to hit the hull of the submarine, which was 25 feet below the surface, but it might by a happy chance have hit the periscope, which would have done as well. As it was, with our slow turning speed the Fritz was able to keep astern, and we were not able to bring anything to bear. The only thing left was a small 40lb. depth charge. At 200 yards, of course, it would not do it any damage, but it might keep it amused for a few minutes, and put off the moment of the firing of its torpedo. So over went the depth charge, and made quite a considerable stir for its size. Unluckily our low speed prevented us from getting altogether out of the sphere of its influence, and when it exploded at a depth of 40 feet the ship got a rude shock which started some of the rivets aft. The submarine did not seem to like it either, and dived. But the evil moment had only been postponed. It was bound to get us in the end, unless something quite unforeseen happened. Yet no one seemed in the least perturbed. The men had the greatest faith in the CO, and waited calmly for orders, sure that he would pull them through somehow. It made an immense difference having a man like that in charge. He was always cool, and cheerful, and inspired every-one with confidence. When things were at their worst he was at his best. On the present occasion, things did not seem bright at that moment, but they were soon to change their aspect, for out of the mist ahead burst HMS *Halcyon* and two 'P' boats, coming along at full speed. The submarine must have heard them on its hydrophone and cleared off, as its periscope was next sighted, sometime later, 3 miles to the southward. Our rescuers did not approach, but zig-zagged about on the horizon, disappearing into mist at one place and coming out of it somewhere else. We wanted to report that there was a submarine around, and to ask for a doctor, but they were too intent in rushing about trying to find something to strafe to pay much attention to us.

At 6.00am the world seemed to hold only a large and aggressive submarine and ourselves, but the place soon began to be thickly populated. In addition to the *Halcyon* and the two 'P' boats, rushing furiously about, three light cruisers with their attendant TBDs came into sight from the east. They swept by at a great pace and passed out of sight in the direction of Harwich. We tried to signal them for a doctor, but they evidently regarded us with suspicion, and took no notice. Hardly had they gone than their place was taken by TBDs from Harwich, dozens of them. They seemed all over the place. It was a stirring and wonderful sight. Wherever one looked some of these graceful craft were dashing along, zig-zagging about at full speed. At that time Zeebrugge TBDs were very troublesome, and the Harwich flotilla was fairly out for their blood. When therefore the *Halcyon* sent in a W/T message that she was making for the sound of firing to the east, the Harwich crowd rushed out, hoping that it was Germans, and were on the spot in less than three quarters of an hour.

With a considerable portion of Britain's light forces round us we could take things easily, and complete the plugging of the shell-hole, pump the ship clear of water and see to the magazine. But first we had to get hold of a doctor. HMS *Torrent* stopped long enough to lower a whaler with a doctor, and then rushed off again, until the boat had collected Ryder and was ready to be hoisted again. The CO and I were glad to see Ryder in the hands of a surgeon, as we feared we had given him too much morphia. One pill did not seem to have any effect, and, as he was in great pain, we gave him another one, and that seemed to have overdone things. Eventually Ryder made a good recovery. The surgeons put a silver plate in to replace the bone. The arm is stiff, but the wonder is that he has an arm at all.

As regards the fire in the magazine, when the place came to be cleared up it was found that a number of patent fire extinguishers which were kept there had all been smashed by the explosion of the shell, and it was supposed that the fumes thus liberated had put out the fire.

Months afterwards we heard that the submarine had photographed us. The curious lump on the end of a stem which had been noticed the first time the periscope appeared was a camera.

Next time we went out one of our own submarines went with us. The idea was that we should sail along in the ordinary way, and that the submarine should follow us submerged. If we were torpedoed the Fritz would very likely come to the surface to contemplate his work, and our mate would then have a good chance of getting it. Again if Fritz attacked us by gun-fire we were to endeavour to draw him towards our submarine, who would be in a good position to attack. A code of signals based on the arrangement of our sails and the position of our flag was agreed on to indicate to our companion the position of the enemy. When cruising in company our submarine usually kept a cable on our quarter showing about 6 inches of periscope. It was most extraordinarily difficult to keep this in sight. It was one man's sole duty to watch it, yet quite half of the time it could not be seen, in spite of the fact that we knew exactly where to look for it. In calm water it could be made out easily, but if there were the least sea it was most difficult to spot. Another difficulty was the question of speed. Lieutenant J——, RN, who was in command of the submarine, wished to cruise at from 1½ to 2 knots, and no more, to avoid running his accumulators down. Perhaps it will be well to explain that, when submerged, submarines do not use their petrol motors on account of the fumes they give off. These are only used on the surface. When submerged, submarines run on electric motors, the electricity, or 'juice' as it is usually called, being stored in accumulators. When following us he had to keep submerged during the hours of daylight, about sixteen out of the twenty-four, and if he had travelled faster than 2 knots he would have used up all the electricity, and have had no reserve in case he had to attack towards the end of the day. At dark he always came to the surface and cruised around, charging up his accumulators by means of the surface petrol motor. Keeping our speed down to his limit was rather a problem in a brisk breeze, and at times we were obliged to go astern on our motor to reduce the pace.

The first night out afforded a little mild sensation, not to us, as we did not know anything about it until the next day, but to our companion, who while cruising around in the dark came upon an enemy submarine on the surface watching the ship. The two sighted each other at the same moment, and both did a crash dive. There was no sequel. They lost each other.

Next day when off Smith's Knoll our submarine came to the surface at midday, owing to trouble with its planes. As soon as they came up J—— semaphored us to say what was the matter, and then occupied himself with the plane. He did not notice two 'P' boats away on the horizon, but they noticed him, swung round, and came racing up at top speed. A submarine alongside a coaster! Dirty work! 'P' boats to the rescue! Meanwhile the submarine people, engrossed with the task in hand, did not see the challenges flashed at them, and were quite unconscious of the approaching danger. We could of course see what was happening, and shouted and made all the noise possible to attract their attention, but without effect. We also tried to signal the 'P' boats, but they had a job on hand and paid no attention. Nearer and nearer they came and then, no reply having been made to the challenge, the leading ship opened fire. Luckily the shell went over. At the sound of the passing shell J—— looked up and gave an order over his shoulder, and then went on with his work. A seaman came up, carefully balanced himself on the conning tower rails, shook out a White Ensign which he had under his arm, and waved it at the 'P' boat. The incident had closed. J—— soon afterwards came alongside to say that he must return to harbour. He made no allusion whatever to having been fired at. His planes were what occupied his mind, and he did not seem to think the other affair worth referring to. The CO expressed his regret at the incident.

'Oh, that,' J—— replied. 'Yes, rotten bad form.'

These submarine officers were the coolest men it is possible to imagine. Nothing, absolutely nothing, ever seemed to ruffle them.

We also returned to land a man whose nerves had given way. He had been blown up right at the start of the war in the drifter *Lindsell*.

HMS *Speedy* was on the spot, and lowered a boat to pick up survivors. As it was returning the *Speedy* herself was blown up. After our last scrap was over, it was reported to me that he was bad. I went to see him, and he said that he was dizzy, and that everything seemed to be turning round. The medicine chest contained only castor oil, black draught, and morphia pills, and I was very doubtful as to which would do him the most good, or perhaps the least harm, and decided in favour of castor oil. I gave him a big dose of this and said confidently that in ten minutes he would be all right, and strangely enough in ten minutes he was all right, but the cure did not last.

A submarine to accompany us was not available until 7 May 1917, and in the meantime we sailed up and down off the coast as before. This keeping to one area was against our wishes. We had so far seen four submarines and had scraps with three of them, all in the same neighbourhood, while no one knows how many may have seen us, and we feared that we were getting too well known. We did not know then that we had actually been photographed. Accordingly the CO asked permission to go to the Channel, or to the West Coast, where we were not known, and might hope to do some good, but permission was refused. Moreover, our orders were to keep to areas outside the traffic lanes, where coasters never went. That alone was enough to give us away. Luckily for us the submarine commanders seemed to have taken the view that as long as they knew who we were we did no harm, while if they sank us the ship would be replaced by another one, which they would not know, and which might sink some of them. Instead of saying: 'Hallo, here is a "Q" ship. Let us sink her,' they seemed to have said: 'Hallo, here is a "Q" ship. Well, we know all about her, and so she cannot do any harm. Leave her alone.'

On 7 May, J—— turned up again with his submarine, and we went off together. On the third day out while submerged he ran into our ship, and bent the periscope, and had to leave us once more.

A few days later another submarine arrived with Lieutenant P——, RN, in charge. On the first night out when we were off Cromer going north a submarine loomed up ahead. Now as far as we knew our submarine was astern, at least it was when last seen. What then was this other one? It had raised bows and looked like a Fritz. The guns were manned. It came by quite close, and then turned and came alongside, and hailed us to ask for the bearing and distance of the Haisbro' Lightship. Our men were itching to fire, but the voice had been without question English, and other English voices could be heard talking in the conning tower. After a question or two, the CO was satisfied that all was in order, and gave the information demanded, Warning them at the same time that there was another British submarine astern. Luckily the two did not meet.

A day or two later P——'s planes also gave out, and he had to go in. After that we had to work alone, no submarine being available. Up and down the coast we sailed, but never saw as much as a periscope, and the CO became convinced that if we were to do any good we must have another ship. This was represented to the authorities on shore, and finally agreed to, but no steamer could be found and our hopes were dashed to the ground. The CO did not want another sailing ship. He was tired of sailing ships, which is not surprising, as he was accustomed to destroyers. I well remember that on one occasion we particularly wanted to get to a certain position at a certain time to meet our submarine. The wind fell light and came ahead, and it was plain that we could not possibly be at the rendezvous in time. The CO came below and flung his cap on the table.

'All I can say,' he said very seriously, 'is that my admiration for Nelson, Collingwood, Howe, and the other great sailing captains is going up by leaps and bounds.'

No steamer or, for the matter of that, no sailing ship being available we were told that we must be content with the one we had, and we went on sailing up and down the east coast, between the parallels of 52° and 54° 30′ N latitude. No submarines, however, appeared to stimulate our drooping spirits, and the CO became desperate. Time was going on, and we were doing no good, and he felt that a supreme effort must be made to pull us out of the rut we were in. He asked for, and obtained, permission to go off and try and find a suitable steamer himself, and had the great luck to find a small steamer which he thought would do right off. He brought back particulars, and his choice was approved. The owners were told that the Admiralty had need of the ship, and that she was to be at Lowestoft by a certain date. She was the last of their little fleet. All their other steamers had been sunk, or taken over by the Admiralty. One of their ships under Commander Day, RNR, had a terrible fight with a German raider *Leopard*. HMS *Achilles*, cruiser, came up while the fight was on and administered the coup de grace. While these arrangements were proceeding, we continued our excursions into the North Sea, with no better luck than before, but we were no longer despondent, as we knew that the other ship would be along soon. As a matter of fact the life itself was very pleasant in fine weather, and it was only the conviction that we should never have another 'show' in that ship as long as we were kept on the East Coast that was depressing. The routine we followed was this. The ship's company, except the cook and the marine who were day men, i.e., worked all day and had all night in, and the W/T operator who went on watch at his instruments at fixed hours, were divided into three watches each under a petty officer or a leading seaman. The men off watch could sleep, read, write, mend clothes, or do what they liked, but they were not allowed to appear on deck. They might sit on the deck below the bulwarks, but were not allowed to stand up or show themselves. The CO and I worked watch and watch, and one of us was always about, not necessarily on deck, as that might have made too many showing, but dressed and awake and within call.

CHAPTER SIX

A FIGHT TO A FINISH

By Lieutenant-Commander Harold Auten, VC

On 30 July 1918, the *Stock Force* had an opportunity of showing her mettle. Early in the morning we were making our way up channel along the northern coast of France.

By this time we had got the crew well drilled, and the nigger (*sic.*) was conspicuously placed, leaning over the rail in the fore end of the well deck, with his pipe in the corner of his mouth. Nothing was anywhere visible, and everything seemed peaceful and quiet. There was hardly a ripple on the water, and somewhere about 8.00am the Island of Guernsey became visible through the morning mist. A little later the sun's rays played on the many glass houses of the island. These were plainly visible from the passing collier, and the day seemed as if it were going to be absolutely ideal.

About 8.15am a signal was intercepted by our concealed wireless, stating that an enemy submarine was working roughly on the line between Casquets to 20 miles south of Start Point (South Devon). Everything seemed to point to this being a good day for an encounter with Fritz. We were in a position where we could alter our course without much suspicion being caused by any watching craft. I accordingly ordered that we steer so as to pass 5 miles south of Lizard Point, thus assuring that we pass right through the area in which the submarine had been reported. The new course tallied with that of a ship bound from Havre to Cardiff.

About 10.00am two French seaplanes came upon the peaceful scene and started to fly about over the ship. First they went ahead, then astern, and finally dropped two messages, which we picked up by our boat. After we had got them on board they turned out to be little red buoys with a tally attached advising us that there was a submarine in the vicinity, and that we had better clear out at once.

Nothing suited us better and we continued to stand on our course, but the two seaplanes were a trouble. They spoilt our game, and we wanted to get rid of them; but there seemed no way to communicate with them without giving ourselves away, so all we could do was to grin and bear it, and pray that they would clear off. That day there was a lot said on the lower deck about seaplanes.

They went ahead and then on the bows. Suddenly several loud explosions occurred. The seaplanes had dropped some bombs on what was evidently an oil slack, but with no apparent result. They hung around and appeared to be convoying the ship. During all this time everybody on board was cursing the seaplanes for all they were worth. 'Why don't they buzz off?' was the remark heard on all sides. The seaplanes, however, thinking that they were doing us a good service, continued to escort us through the danger zone. This went on for several hours, the ship steering her course, the two French seaplanes escorting us.

At noon one of the seaplanes alighted on the water. By this time I was thoroughly fed up with them and wished them further. The day was ideal for the work in which we were engaged, and all we wanted was to be left to ourselves. The Frenchmen, however, were apparently worked up to such a state of excitement that they would have dropped a bomb on a sprat had it appeared.

The seaplane that had alighted on the water appeared to have something wrong with it, so I altered my course to render any assistance I could, and also to tell him to clear out. Before we could reach her, however, she had risen again, and then, the pair of them, after a valedictory circling around the ship, made off for the coast of France, satisfied in their own minds that they had saved a very stupid and dull-witted, not to say dirty little craft from her fate.

The ship continued to plough her way on towards the supposed destination, and all through the afternoon a specially good look-out was kept. The first dog watch-keepers relieved the afternoon watch from their trying duties, and these continued to keep a good look-out, realising that anywhere on this peaceful scene might lurk a 'U' boat.

The officer on watch was walking up and down the bridge giving a keen glance round when he came to each wing of the bridge.

Suddenly, when looking over the starboard side, he saw a commotion in the water some considerable distance away.

After gazing at it intently for a second, wondering if it were a school of porpoises, he saw that it was the track of a torpedo coming direct for the ship. He instantly struck the alarm, at the same time ordering the helm to be put hard over and the engines full speed astern. At this moment the majority of those on board were having tea, the officers being seated in the saloon discussing the events of the morning.

One and all quickly and quietly got to our stations. I reached the bridge just in time to see the torpedo, then about 50 yards off, coming direct for the ship. She was coming very slowly in the end, having been fired at a long range and appearing to have very nearly run her distance. It looked to everybody on the bridge as if the torpedo would pass ahead; but suddenly, to my amazement, it took a turn in towards the ship and struck us abreast of No. 1 hatch.

The damage done was indescribable. The ship was only 161 feet over all, with a beam of 29 feet, and the torpedo had hit direct on the second watertight bulkhead, forcing it clean through the other side of the ship. The forward end of the bridge went entirely, and all I recollected was going up in the air, and coming down to find myself underneath the chart table. Probably, if I had been a light-weight, the chart table would have won.

The whole fore deck was bent, derricks were blown overboard, and up went an awful shower of flotation planks, unexploded 12-pounder shells and debris caused by the explosion. This lot came down again with an awful clatter, wounding all the people on the bridge except myself, by virtue of having won the race with the chart table.

Immediately after this came down a huge deluge of water that had been thrown up by the explosion. This drenched us all to the skin and, combined with the explosion, caused many who were in the vicinity to become violently sick.

I asked one of the men on the bridge afterwards what he really thought had happened at that moment.

'Well, sir,' he said, ' if you really want to know, I thought the end of the world had come.'

My first thought on recovering myself was, 'I wonder how many men have been lost,' and getting up from beneath the wreckage, I surveyed the damage forward. Just at that moment I caught sight of the nigger, and he was in such a condition that I really had to roar with laughter.

Stowed in the forward end of the hatch was a quantity of paint. This had all gone up on the air with the explosion. The nigger had stepped from beneath the forecastle just in time to receive the full benefit of a big tin of white paint, and instead of being black, he was white. At the moment I caught sight of him he was trying to get the paint out of his eyes. He looked a beautiful sight, and no one would have taken him for a nigger, which was the role I wanted him for in the 'panic party'.

As soon as we had recovered ourselves, the officers and the crew on the bridge hurriedly went to their stations, while I went down to find out the number of our casualties. To my intense surprise I discovered that there had been nobody killed, which was marvellous, considering that some of the men were going to their stations right alongside where the torpedo had exploded, and yet had escaped with their lives.

A number were wounded, and these were quickly got down on to the 'tween deck. On looking round I found one poor fellow, an officers' steward named Starling, pinned in a mass of wreckage underneath a 12-pounder gun. It would have taken a working party an hour to get him out, and time was valuable.

The ship was settling down by the head, and I wondered how long she was going to float, so I told him that he would have to remain where he was for the present, and we would get him out at the first possible opportunity. On my telling him this he said quite cheerfully, 'All right, sir, I'll lay quiet until you let me know.'

I asked him some time afterwards what he recollected of this event.

'Well, sir,' he said, 'I lay quiet there after you had left and the "abandon ship party" had gone, and the first thing that I remember was the black cat making her way forward.'

The water had risen considerably and the cat, it appeared, had been blown up in the explosion, and had ended up by being buried beneath some debris and in the water. She had managed to extricate herself from this, and the steward watched her get up on the top of a plank, very carefully shake herself like a dog, and then, with her hair all standing on end, her tail up, start to pick her way gingerly and carefully over the debris to a dry spot.

After having got the wounded down on the 'tween deck, which by this time was also filling rapidly with water, we manned the two after 4-inch guns, which were luckily all right, except that the tremendous column of water had smashed in the roof of the foremost one. The guns' crews, however, immediately got up some oars as props, so that everything from the outward appearance appeared quite natural.

The 'panic party', who had been carrying out their theatrical performance, were then ordered to shove off. The wounded were now locked down in the 'tween deck, where the surgeon, above his knees in water, worked and attended to their injuries. They were shut down like rats in a trap, and could not possibly have escaped had the ship foundered.

The steward was lying pinned in the range end of the fore-gun, the two after guns' crews were lying on their stomachs waiting for what was to happen, while the engine-room staff remained at their posts. The ship was settling rapidly by the head, and at one time I felt she would not last much longer, but the wood which had been so splendidly stowed kept us up.

The 'abandon ship party' pulled off on to the port bow, where they lay waiting for what would happen. The fore end of the ship having been entirely shattered, voice-pipes and wire reel control gone, the only place left from which to control the ship was the after gun house, from which I could see nearly all round except right ahead.

Luckily the voice-pipes between the two guns remained intact, so that I was able to communicate with the others.

Everybody lay quiet on board the poor little ship, which by this time had practically her forecastle submerged. Everywhere the water was rising rapidly except in the engine room, which, being in the stern, remained comparatively dry. We were all keyed up to a state of high tension. We knew the submarine was hanging about watching our every movement through her periscope. If anyone had made the slightest mistake, betraying the fact that there was any one on board, it would have meant another torpedo, and then good-bye to us all.

After having carefully surveyed the ship through her periscope, the submarine came to the surface about half a mile off and lay there. Two men appeared on the conning tower intently watching the ship for any suspicious movement.

After they had scrutinised us for some fifteen minutes, they were evidently almost satisfied, and started to go slowly towards the boat. The 'abandon ship party' then pulled slowly down the port side of the *Stock Force* about 300 yards off.

The submarine was still carefully surveying the ship. When she got down on to the port bow, about 400 yards distant, she stopped again and watched the ship. She was a very shy bird.

Now was coming the critical moment. Everybody on board lay absolutely quiet and hardly daring to breathe. After this scrutiny the submarine appeared to be quite satisfied, and came very slowly down the port bow of the ship, following the boat, which by this time had got in a position where, if the submarine approached her, she would be in the range of both guns.

The submarine came on slowly, awfully slowly. It seemed ages before she got on the beam where both the 4-inch guns could bear. Time after time the after-gunner and myself peeped through the little crack we were using as an observation position, but, no, the submarine was not yet in a satisfactory position to open fire on her. At last she reached the fatal spot.

'Submarine bearing, red 90, range 300 yards, stand by,' I whispered through the voice-pipes; then, a second or so later, 'Let go.'

Down fell the shutters of both guns with a crash. I started violently at the noise. It must have been the surprise of her life for the submarine. The after 4-inch gun being stowed on the port beam, was right on the bearing when the flaps went down, and her first shot passed over the top of the conning tower, bringing down the periscope and wireless. The second shot hit the conning tower, and from reports afterwards received from the 'abandon ship party', who were about 70 yards ahead of the submarine, shifted this bodily on one side and blew one man, evidently the commanding officer, into the air.

By this time the forward 4-inch gun had trained round, and her first shot hit on the hull of the submarine, just below the conning tower. After this shot the submarine seemed to shake herself and she sank a little by the stem, the bows coming up to a corresponding angle. A lot of loose smoke, and what appeared to be steam, began to pour out of her. The first shot from the forward gun had evidently exploded inside the submarine. She now presented a large immobile target into which shell after shell was poured. Gradually she sank by the stern, her bows coming right up out of the water.

During this time the 'abandon ship party' were in a splendid position to see the effect of the ship's firing, being at the most only about 70 yards ahead of the submarine. When the flaps went down, the white ensign went up and the first gun fired, they got up in the boat and yelled themselves hoarse, waving their caps and cheering time after time until the Hun sank.

The effect of the firing had evidently disturbed the trim of the *Stock Force*. After the submarine had sank she started to take a big list to starboard, and it became apparent that she saw no reason to keep afloat much longer now her work was accomplished. The 'abandon ship party' was recalled, and after they had been picked up, we started to get under way to try and close the land and, if possible, beach her.

All the compasses had gone in the explosion. We were also in a critical condition. There were a number of wounded on board the ship, the wireless had gone, and there were no means of getting into communication with any one, or of steering except by sun and wind.

Our first task after the submarine had sunk, was the rescuing of the rating who had been lying pinned underneath the forward gun. He uttered no word of complaint during the awful period of waiting for the submarine to be lured into the position where the *Stock Force*'s guns could bear.

All hands turned to with a will, for the water had crept nearly up to him. However we got him safely out, but in an unconscious condition. Immediately after this the rest of the wounded, who had been put down on the 'tween deck, which by now had nearly 3 feet of water on it, were got up on the main hatch, so that they could be better attended to by the doctor.

After this every man who was able to started with hand pumps, buckets, in fact, anything that would hold water, to bail. The boat accommodation was not sufficient for all of us, so another small party started to construct rafts. Despite our efforts, the water gained rapidly, which taking into consideration that there was a 40-foot hole in the little ship, was hardly to be wondered at. It was the timber which had been so tightly packed in her that kept her afloat so long, and had so materially helped to gain the victory over the Hun.

The bulkhead between the stoke-hold and the engine room had started, and despite every effort made to shore it up and stop the leaks, it continued to make water fast.

A little later on, to everyone's intense relief, a smudge of smoke was sighted on the port bow, Presently two little trawlers came on the scene, their attention having been drawn by the sound of our gunfire. One was immediately ordered alongside, to which was transferred the wounded and part of the ship's company. Two of the officers and myself stayed on board with a small volunteer crew to attempt if possible to save the ship.

The stoke-hold and the engine room staff worked on down below, until the fires were put out by the rapidly rising water, and then the chief engineer secured the boilers and came on deck.

The ship now started to heel over to starboard, until she floated the starboard lifeboat at the davit head. It became obvious that her last moments were coming. Accordingly, the rest of the crew, with the exception of the first lieutenant and myself, were got away in the lifeboat.

A little previous to this two small torpedo boats had come upon the scene. One of them put down a small boat and sent over to rescue us both. The first lieutenant and myself got out on to the port side and sat on the rubbing streak, not liking to leave the ship that we had fitted out, and for which we entertained such an affection. It was no good, however. She was going, and was now practically lying on her side. We therefore got into the dinghy and were put on board the TB.

A minute or so afterwards the poor little *Stock Force* sank to her last home. She had been torpedoed 27 miles from the shore, and it was particularly hard to have got her almost within sight of land – the shore was only 8 miles away – and then to lose her.

We all landed at Devonport early the next morning. The wounded were carted away to the hospital, where they were carefully attended to. The remainder of the crew, many of them suffering from shock, were accommodated in the barracks.

I should like to say a few words about the behaviour of my officers and crew. It was beyond all praise. Their coolness and courage throughout the action were worthy of the best traditions of the British Navy. Although many of them were suffering from wounds, and others from the tremendous shock sustained through the torpedo striking so small a ship, everyone went about their duties, which included lying doggo for a full forty minutes on the part of the gun crews, and later stoking in a stoke-hold fast filling with water; all this was done as if exercising their quarters. The success of this action was due to their splendid behaviour.

A few extracts from the Commander-in-Chief's covering letter and the Secretary of the Admiralty's reply will be of interest:

ADMIRAL TO ADMIRALTY. – 'This is one of the best examples of coolness, discipline and good organization that I have ever come across. Number one hold was a huge gash in a little ship, and yet everybody went to their stations as usual. None gave the ship away by a careless or stupid movement or action. When the smallness of the ship and the force of the explosion are considered, it is hard to understand how the officers and men could have stood the shock so well.'

SECRETARY of THE ADMIRALTY TO ADMIRAL. – 'I am to acquaint you that their Lordships concur in your high opinion of the coolness, discipline and good organization in this action, and I am to request that an expression of their appreciation may be conveyed to all concerned. I am further to inform you that the King has been pleased to approve of the following honours to officers and men for their services on this occasion.'

This list included the awarding of a Conspicuous Gallantry Medal to the rating who had lain under the gun, and no one more richly deserved it.

CHAPTER SEVEN

THE ATTACK ON THE MOLE AND AFTER

By Captain A.F.B. Carpenter, VC, RN

The main points of the plan for the blocking of Zeebrugge were as follows: The expedition was to cross the seas during the afternoon and evening, stopping for a few minutes about 20 miles from its destination for the purpose of disembarking the surplus crews of the block-ships. At about this time the first of the diversions, in the form of aerial attacks, were to commence, to be shortly followed by the opening of the long-range bombardments. Meanwhile the expedition, working to a prearranged time table, was to approach the coast.

At given intervals during the approach small craft were to be detached to carry out the duties of smoke screening, of diversionary attacks, of locating the destination and of dealing with enemy vessels which might emerge from their harbours or which were already at sea.

Immediately following the long-range bombardment, the storming vessels, having located the Mole, were to proceed alongside the high outer wall and land their storming parties over it to attack the Mole batteries – this constituting the main diversion of the enterprise. A few minutes later the submarines, having steamed into place beneath the railway viaduct, were to blow up the railway. Twenty minutes after the storming vessels were due to arrive alongside, the blockships were to pass round the end of the Mole, and were to make their dash for the canal entrance, running the gauntlet of the shore batteries, whilst the Mole attack was in full swing. On arriving in the canal the blockers were to turn and sink their ships across the navigable channel. Rescue craft were to follow the blockships for the purpose of rescuing the crews of the latter. Meanwhile, various diversions, smoke screening and the work of the inshore supports, were to be continued sufficiently long to enhance the chances of the rescue. After an hour or so from the commencement of the attack on the Mole all forces were to withdraw.

The break of dawn on 22 April 1918, the first of the seven days of our tabulated period, found many anxious individuals on deck discussing the chances. There was an almost entire absence of wind; the sea was consequently as smooth as the proverbial mill-pond. The general feeling amongst us was that of straining-at-the-leash. We had suffered two major disappointments during the previous period, but we instinctively felt that we had now arrived at a period of maximum anxiety – we knew that the coming week would settle the matter once and for all. Presently light airs from the northward began to catspaw the glassy surface and to increase in frequency and strength until they settled down to a real northerly breeze. Our hopes ran high, but the matter of visibility still claimed our attention. There was the usual early morning mist; this was quickly dispelled when the sun rose above the horizon. It soon became evident that our hopes for misty weather were to be denied us. By 8.00am the visibility was extreme, as they say in meteorological circles; one's horizontal range of vision from ship-board was only limited by one's height of eye above the level of the sea. This condition, to say the least of it, was disconcerting.

It would be high tide at Zeebrugge and Ostend soon after midnight. Arrival at such an hour would entail making much of the oversea passage in broad daylight, and this, as previously mentioned, would in turn lead to grave risk of being seen by the German patrols, whether the latter were in the air, on the sea surface, or submerged keeping periscope watch. Although this disadvantage might even lose us the element of surprise on which we had concentrated so much effort, any postponement of our departure until the morrow would entail a reduction of our available period by one-seventh. The armchair critic who knows nought of such matters cannot easily conceive either the difficulty of arriving at such decisions, or the weight of responsibility which lies on the shoulders of the man by whom the decision must be given.

Early in the forenoon it was evident that all conditions except visibility were in favour of starting our third attempt. Our hopes ran high in spite of the fact that previous experience had shown us how fickle the weather could be. Somehow we felt that our chance had come at last.

We were in telephonic communication with Dover via a lighthouse in the vicinity of our anchorage. Perhaps the word 'communication' rather exaggerates the actual facts. The line apparently passed through a certain holiday resort whose telephone exchange was below par and whose operator, in the kindness of her heart, generally managed to connect at least four persons simultaneously on our particular line. The resulting cross-talk, further confused by the eternal argument between the tidal stream and the telephone cable, and our impatience at any and every interruption, with its resultant increase of knowledge of the vernacular to the lighthouse crew, were hardly conducive to easy conversation on important matters.

'Harold' was particularly exasperating that morning. Having fixed 'Mabel' for lunch in a couple of hours, he apparently thought it necessary to 'phone her details of his past'.

To the Vice-Admiral at Dover fell the responsibility of deciding whether we should start or not. After a discussion on the telephone the die was cast – we were ordered to 'proceed in execution of previous orders.' The order was passed to the ships and the requisite preparations were put in hand immediately. We raised steam without delay. Baggage, final letters, and all unnecessary paraphernalia were disembarked. Once again determination and expectancy had expanded into enthusiasm. The time for 'action' had arrived.

I do not think we had any feelings of anxiety now except with regard to the weather. Surely nothing would prevent the culmination of all our hopes at this eleventh hour. No suggestion of failure ever occurred to us. Our confidence in the face of the many obstacles, when considered in cold blood months afterwards, may have seemed to be almost an impertinence. Everybody knew exactly what was expected of them. There was no actual excitement except that inseparable from intense enthusiasm. Last-minute orders or signals were not required, everything worked just as smoothly as if we had been merely starting off on a picnic.

Engines were reported 'ready' shortly after lunch. Just before weighing anchor I had gone below to don my sea-boots and other appropriate 'togs'; on reappearing on deck I found several officers grouped for a final snapshot and was requested to join them. Alas, that was indeed the last photograph for several of them. The cheering which had taken place on the previous attempts was indulged in once again as the ships proceeded to sea and was only eclipsed by the cheers which welcomed the survivors to Dover on the following day.

Of the earlier part of the oversea trip little need be written. *Vindictive* took *Iris* and *Daffodil* in tow and was closely followed by the blockships. In due course the Dover forces were sighted; the combined force, accompanied by aeroplanes, formed on *Vindictive*, which was 'Guide of the Fleet.'

The fast motor boats and the two submarines were taken in tow, and the Vice-Admiral, with his flag flying in the destroyer *Warwick*, directed the whole movements and gave the signal to proceed as soon as all were formed up. The visibility had already decreased and sufficient clouds were massing overhead to revive our anxieties about the weather. Light squadrons which had preceded us for the various duties of 'supporting' or 'bombarding', etc., had not reported any enemy patrol craft.

On board each ship eleventh-hour preparations were being made such as rigging stations for attending the wounded, distributing first-aid packages, passing hoses along in case of fire, fusing bombs and shells, testing electric circuits, providing candle lamps in case of electrical failures, grouping ammunition round the guns, donning clean underclothing as a guard against septic wounds, darkening ship to prevent any warning of our approach, placing spare charts in alternative positions, testing smoke screen apparatus and flame throwers, and many other such things.

Before darkness set in a signal was received from the Vice-Admiral reading 'St George for England.' It was reported to me as being a personal signal to myself, but I subsequently ascertained that it was intended as a general signal to be passed down the line of ships. It was made in the semaphore code from *Warwick* and has often been mis-quoted as a signal hoisted with alphabetical flags.

One garbled version described the signal as having been 'flashed to all ships just before reaching the Mole.' This story of a flash-light having been used just when the ships were endeavouring to take the enemy by surprise under cover of darkness is really too fantastic to pass uncontradicted. Believing it to be a private signal a reply was determined upon. The reply to the Admiral's signal ('May we give the Dragon's tail a damned good twist.'), judged by the ordinary standards, was somewhat impertinent, but impertinence was in the air that afternoon. Incidentally my signalman substituted the word 'darned' for 'damned' and, when corrected, spelt the word 'dammed' as a compromise.

Our prearranged time-table had laid down the exact minute at which we were to pass through certain lettered positions, the latter being marked by buoys placed by the surveying officers. Position G was to be the parting of the ways, namely, the position at which the

The *Cap Trafalgar* was a German passenger liner converted to an auxiliary cruiser in the middle of August 1914 at the remote Brazilian island of Trinidada. Her third funnel, a dummy, was removed to disguise her identity. Armed with two 4.1 inch guns and six one-pounder pom-poms, manned by experienced naval personnel her mission was to sink British merchant shipping. Spotted at Trinidada by the British, a two-hour engagement resulted in both ships being severely shot-up. *Carmania* was listing severely, flooding and burning when the *Cap Trafalgar* heeled over to port and sank rapidly.

The *Carmania*, although on fire and flooding, was rescued the next day by units of the Royal Navy and towed to Pernambuco.

HMS *Audacious* was a King George V-class battleship. She was sunk by a mine laid by the auxiliary minelayer *Berlin*, off the northern coast of Donegal, Ireland, on 27 October, 1914. Fortunately the RMS *Olympic* was close by to help rescue the crew.

The RMS *Olympic* was a transatlantic ocean liner: the lead ship of the White Star Line. Her maiden voyage was on 14 June 1911. Both her sister ships sank, the *Titanic* after hitting an iceberg, and the *Britannic* after hitting a mine on 21 November 1916. The *Olympic* was scrapped in 1935. During the war she was a troopship. The razzle dazzle camouflage was designed to break up the ship's shape making it difficult for a U-boat commander to estimate a target's range, speed and heading.

The crew of *Audacious* took to lifeboats and were rescued by RMS *Olympic*. The photo was taken by Mabel and Edith Smith of Derby, passengers on the *Olympic*, returning from America.

HMS *Warrior* was a Warrior-class armoured cruiser launched in 1905. From December 1914 she was part of the Grand Fleet and was part of the British naval forces at Jutland where she was heavily damaged. She was 'later abandoned and sank in a rising sea.'

HMS *Queen Mary* at sea with her torpedo net booms folded against her side. She was the last battlecruiser built for the Royal Navy before the war and was commissioned on 4 September 1913. During the Battle of Jutland she was hit twice by the German battlecruiser *Derfflinger* and her magazines exploded shortly afterwards sinking the ship.

A German photograph showing the final minutes of the Battle Cruiser *Queen Mary*. Among the casualties was Lieutenant Victor Ewart, the only son of Major-General Sir Henry Ewart. Born on 15 February 1891 he was a godchild of Queen Victoria. A career naval officer he died caring for others. A survivor from the turret he commanded during the battle stated 'he not only fought his guns to the last, but gave up what little chance he had of escape by turning back to search the turret and ammunition rooms for men.'

SMS *Frauenlob* was a German light cruiser sunk at the battle of Jutland.

HMS *Vindictive* was an Arrogant-class cruiser launched in 1897. Obsolescent at the start of the war she served in the south Atlantic and White Sea. Early in 1918 she was fitted out for the Zeebrugge raid. She was sunk as a blockship on 10 May 1918 at Ostend. The wreck was raised in 1920 and the bow section preserved as a memorial.

An aerial view of two British ships sunk in Zeebrugge harbour.

German heavy bombers taking off for a raid. The Gotha, designed for long-range service, was principally used for night bombing but was also used for day bombing.

Manfred von Richthofen, the Red Baron, seated in the cockpit of the Albatross 111, with members of *Jasta* 11 in 1917. His younger brother Lothar is sat at the front of the group.

Jadgstaffel 11 lined up ready for a patrol. The Red Baron flew a bright red Albatross D.III more often than he flew the Fokker Dr.1 with which he is usually associated.

French troops on Gallipoli before an attack on 21 June 1915. These are North African troops with European officers.

Some of the many wounded that were evacuated from Gallipoli and sent to Egypt or Malta to recover. These men are being embarked from a hospital ship on lighters to get them to shore.

A BE2c (Bleriot Experimental) was initially constructed for stability at a time when reconnaissance was considered one of the most important roles in aviation. It was a two-seater which became one of the longest serving and multi-functional aircraft of the first world war. Although reviled by many for its rear-placed pilot's cockpit, limited gunners space and engine problems, the BE2 was used for anything from artillery spotting to reconnaissance, bombing missions, anti-zeppelin attacks and transport.

Hauptmann Oswald Boelcke was a German flying ace, with forty credited victories, was one of the most influential patrol leaders and tacticians of the early years of air combat. He was killed in combat at the age of 25 on 28 October 1916.

forces destined for the inshore attacks on Zeebrugge and Ostend should separate en route for their respective destinations. That position was so chosen that the forces should arrive at their destinations simultaneously, making due allowance for direction and strength of the tidal stream and for actual ship-speed through the water. This idea of simultaneous operations at the two places was not the only important factor for consideration; it was also necessary that all other phases of the attack, such as long-range bombardments and aerial attacks, should synchronise with the movements of the blockships. It was, therefore, necessary to either work exactly to schedule as laid down in the time-table or else inform all units of any change in the zero time; the latter being the minute at which *Vindictive* should pass through position G. This in turn necessitated forecasting the zero time as a result of the observed times of passing the previous positions. We had left position a few minutes ahead of time and passed through position D with barely a minute in hand. 'No alteration of zero time' was therefore communicated to all units.

After passing position D the whole assembly of vessels stopped for a few minutes for the triple purpose of disembarking surplus blockship crews, for ascertaining the exact direction of wind (this information being required for the use of the smoke screens), and for re-forming into 'approach order' after casting off the tow of the submarines and small craft. It was then pitch dark, the moon being entirely obscured by clouds. It has been stated elsewhere that the *Intrepid* did not disembark any of her surplus crews. The small vessel detailed to take these men failed to appear owing to a breakdown; this must have pleased the *Intrepid*'s surplus crew who, it will be remembered, had shown a strong disinclination to leave their ship. To some extent *Thetis* and *Iphigenia* were similarly placed; history relates that when the small vessels arrived alongside many members of the surplus crews could not be found, so anxious were they to complete the operation which they had begun so well.

No time was lost in reforming the squadron and we started off again for position G. At about this time all conditions to wind and sea were still favourable, but slight rain had begun of fall and to reduce the already very limited visibility. The rain thus provided the first of the incidents which could not be foreseen.

The result of the rain was twofold. Firstly, it somewhat delayed the commencement of the long-range bombardment on Zeebrugge owing to the reduction in visibility rendering the monitor's position doubtful.

Secondly, and far more important, it acted very adversely against the use of aircraft. The difficulty and danger of flying in wet weather is too well known to need enlargement here, but the difficulty of locating the positions which were to be bombed was enormously increased. Our aerial bombers had made a magnificent attack on the occasion of our first attempt and they had become none the less determined to render a good account of themselves when the operation finally took place. Imagine their intense disappointment. It was not difficult for those who knew the splendid work of our Air Force to realise that they would stop at nothing to achieve their object. In spite of all the difficulties it is impossible to conceive of greater determination than was shown, but the rain rendered the attack impossible. The losses amongst these very gallant airmen amounted to a high percentage of those who started on their errand.

At position G the Ostend blockships, *Sirius* and *Brilliant*, parted company; inwardly, we wished them the best of luck.

The main portion of the oversea passage having been completed the 'Approach' now commenced.

II

After zero-time the remaining units kept in close company until such times as each, according to their respective instructions, was deputed to proceed independently to carry out their several duties.

The force was preceded by the Vice-Admiral in *Warwick* with some half a dozen other craft in company ready to fall upon and destroy any enemy patrol vessels which might be encountered. We were now steaming through the German mined areas and were hoping against hope that no mines would be touched to the main detriment of the element of surprise. If any mine had exploded the enemy could not have failed to have their suspicions aroused. The rain gradually increased and the wind became more fitful.

Hot soup was distributed to the men in *Vindictive* at about 10.30pm and a 'tot' of rum about an hour later to those who desired it.

About fifty minutes before midnight the hawser with which *Vindictive* was towing *Iris* and *Daffodil* suddenly parted. It was then too late to retake these vessels in tow and, indeed, it would have been a difficult and dangerous task in the rain and inky darkness with so many vessels in close company, to say nothing of the loss of time and the obstacle to accurate navigation. Speed had to be somewhat eased temporarily to allow *Vindictive* to drop back to her original position relative to the other vessels. In accordance with the plan the blockships eased speed for the purpose of arriving at the Mole some twenty minutes after *Vindictive*.

We were momentarily expecting to meet the German patrol vessels and to be discovered from the shore. Suddenly a light-buoy was seen. A hurried bearing laid down on the chart agreed exactly with the reported position of a buoy off Blankenberge. Incidentally a captured prisoner had recently stated that this buoy had been withdrawn or moved elsewhere, but we had promulgated its original position to all concerned because we suspected that this particular individual was a disciple of Ananias. This agreement between our position by 'dead-reckoning' and that of the buoy was decidedly heartening, for we had obtained no 'fix' for several miles and were running through a cross tidal stream of doubtful strength.

The difficulties attached to forecasting the movements of tidal streams was borne out in the case of the bombarding monitors, HMS *Erebus* and *Terror*. In addition to being somewhat hampered by the low visibility resulting from the rain, these vessels, on arrival at their firing positions, discovered that the tidal stream was flowing in exactly the opposite direction to that anticipated; this, in turn, caused some delay in opening fire, but, as events subsequently showed, the delay was of no great consequence. The bombardment was carried out without any further hitch. The Germans do not appear to have been able to locate the monitors until the firing was nearly completed. The few German shells which burst in the vicinity of the firing ships were doubtless directed by some means of sound-ranging and direction-finding. On finishing the bombardment the monitors took up their positions for covering the subsequent retirement of the attacking forces.

It may be stated here that, barring the impossibility of aerial attack, the delay in commencing the long-range bombardment and the part-ing of the towing hawser, there was no hitch of any kind sufficient to alter the general idea of the enterprise. Everything was carried out to schedule time. Soon after passing the Blankenberge light-buoy the enemy appeared to suspect that something more than a bombardment was afoot. Star shells were fired to seaward and searchlights were switched on. That was exactly what we had hoped for. If only they would continue to illuminate the atmosphere our navigational diffi-culties would be enormously reduced. The star shells were extra-ordinary. They burst with a loud report just overhead and lit up our surroundings to the maximum of the then visibility. Much to our surprise no enemy vessels were encountered or even seen; presumably the enemy set the greater dependence on their mines.

To the southward – namely between us and the shore our smoke-screeners had laid down a 'pea-soup' fog. Nothing was to be seen in that direction except the glare of searchlights and of gun flashes, the latter being presumably directed against the fast motor boats which had run into the anchorage behind the Mole for the purpose of torpedoing vessels secured alongside. At this stage the wind died away completely and the rain was heavier than ever.

In *Vindictive* we took up our action stations. Our battery guns had been instructed not to open fire until it was certain that our individual presence had been discovered. The guns in the lighting-top on our foremast were in readiness to engage. Rocket men had been stationed to fire illuminating flares for the purpose of locating the Mole. The storming parties were under cover awaiting the order to storm the Mole. The cable party were in the forecastle standing by to drop anchor at the foot of the high wall. Other parties with wire hawsers were stationed to assist the *Daffodil* in her important task of pushing *Vindictive* bodily alongside. Crews were standing by the bomb-mortars and flame-throwers for clearing the Mole before sending the stormers over the wall. The Engineering and Stokehold personnel were at their stations below for giving immediate response to all requirements from the conning positions. The first-lieutenant, Lieutenant-Commander R.R. Rosoman, RN, was in the conning tower, from where the ship was being steered by the quartermaster, in readiness to take over the handling of the ship immediately I was rendered *hors de combat*. It was a decidedly tense period, but there were others to follow.

At a given moment by watch-time *Vindictive* altered course towards the Mole, or rather towards the position where it was hoped to find the Mole. Almost immediately we ran into the smoke screen. The wind had now changed to an off-shore direction, diametrically opposite to that on which the screening plans had been based. I thought at the time that this smoke screen was the thickest on record – that opinion was changed later.

The visibility at this time can hardly have amounted to a yard – the forecastle was invisible from the bridge. The firing of star shells and guns, and the flashing of searchlights became more frequent. *Vindictive* was being conned from the flame-thrower hut on the port end of the conning tower platform. This position was especially suitable in that it plumbed over the ship's side and thus provided a very good outlook for berthing at the Mole. There was a curious absence of excitement. Even the continued repetition of the question: 'Are you all right, sir?' from my first-lieutenant, a prearranged idea to ensure a quick change-over of command, became monotonous. Nothing had yet been seen of the Mole from *Vindictive*. This comparatively quiet period was not of long duration.

III

A few seconds before the schedule time for the last alteration of course, designed to take us alongside the outer wall, the smoke screen, which had been drifting northwards before the new wind, suddenly cleared. Barely 300 yards distant, dead ahead of us, appeared a long, low, dark object which was immediately recognised as the Mole itself, with the lighthouse at its extremity. We had turned up heading direct for the six-gun battery exactly as arranged in the plan. Those who know aught of navigation will realise how far this was a fluke. Probably the various errors in compass direction, allowance for tide, etc., had exactly cancelled one another. Course was altered immediately to the south-westwards and speed was increased to the utmost.

The Mole battery opened fire at once; our own guns, under the direction of Commander E.O.B.S. Osborne, replied with the utmost promptitude. The estimated distances at which we passed the Mole battery was 250 yards off the eastern gun, gradually lessening to 50 yards off the western gun. It was truly a wonderful sight. The noise was terrific, and the flashes of the Mole guns seemed to be within arm's length. Of course it was, to all intents and purposes, impossible for the Mole guns to miss their target. They literally poured projectiles into us. In about five minutes we had reached the Mole, but not before the ship had suffered a great amount of damage to both *materiel* and personnel.

Looked at from the view of a naval officer it was little short of criminal, on the part of the Mole battery, that the ship was allowed to reach her destination. Everything was in favour of the defence as soon as we had been sighted. Owing to the change of wind our special arrangements for covering the battery with smoke had failed in spite of the magnificent work of our small smoke vessels which, unsupported and regardless of risk, had laid the screen close to the foot of the wall, that is to say, right under the muzzles of the guns. From the moment when we were first sighted until arriving alongside the Mole the battery guns had a clear target, illuminated by star shell, of a size equal to half the length of the lighthouse extension itself.

To my mind the chief reasons for our successful running of the gauntlet were twofold, firstly, the fact that we were so close, and secondly, the splendid manner in which our guns' crews stuck to their work. With regard to the former, a longer range would have entailed more deliberate firing, and this in turn would have given time for more deliberate choice of point of aim. A few projectiles penetrating the engine or boiler rooms or holing us at the waterline would have settled the matter. The range being so short one can conjecture that the German gunners, realising that they could not miss, pumped ammunition into us at the utmost speed of which their guns were capable, without regard to the particular damage which they were likely to cause. Their loss of serenity, due in the first place to the novel circumstances of the case, must have been considerably augmented by the fact that our own projectiles were hitting the wall near the gun muzzles – it was too much to hope that we should actually obtain any hits on the guns themselves.

The petty officer at one of our 6-inch guns, when asked afterwards what ranges he fired at, said that he reckoned he opened fire at about 200 yards, and he continued till close to the Mole. 'How close?' he was asked. 'Reckoning from the gun muzzle,' he replied, 'I should say it was about 3 feet.'

One can picture the situation as seen from the Mole itself. A hostile vessel suddenly looming out of the fog at point-blank range, the intense excitement which resulted, the commencement of fire, the bursting of shell on the wall, the ardent desire to hit something as rapidly and as often as possible, the natural inclination to fire at the nearest object – namely, that part of the vessel on their own level, and the realisation that in a few moments the guns would no longer bear on the target. One can imagine the thoughts that were uppermost in their minds: 'Hit her, smash her, pump it in, curse those guns of hers, don't lose a second of time, blow her to bits!'

One cannot blame those gunners. To use a war-time expression, 'They had the wind up.' We had counted on that, we had concentrated all our efforts at 'putting the wind up.' Yet if anybody had seriously suggested that a ship could steam close past a shore battery in these modern days of gunnery he would have been laughed to scorn. Yet it was easy. The reason is not far to seek.

Those who worship *materiel* have followed a false god. The crux of all fighting lies with the personnel – a fact borne out again and again on this particular night just as throughout past history. If the German gunners had been superhuman this tale would not have been told, but human nature, reckoned with by the attackers, was on our side; the initiative was ours.

The material damage was very great, but, though it may sound paradoxical, of not much importance. The upper works and upper deck of the ship received the brunt of it. The most serious matter was the damage to our gangways. Several were shot away and many others damaged beyond further usefulness and, so far as could be observed at the time, only four were left us for the work in hand. Two heavy shells penetrated the ship's side below the upper deck. One passed in just beneath the foremost flame-thrower hut and burst on impact. The other came through within a few feet of the first and wrecked everything in its vicinity. Two other heavy shells came through the screen door to the forecastle and placed one of the howitzer guns out of action. The funnels, ventilators, bridges, charthouse, and all such were riddled through and through.

The damage to the personnel was exceedingly serious. Orders had been given that the storming parties should remain below, under cover, until the ship arrived alongside. The number of personnel in exposed positions was to be limited mainly to those manning the guns, rocket apparatus and flame-throwers. The senior officers of the storming parties, however, stationed themselves in the most handy position for leading and directing the assault, with the result that they were exposed to the full blast of the hurricane fire from the Mole battery. Military officers had always acted in a similar manner whatever their instructions might be. One cannot help feeling that in any fighting service, where discipline is based on leadership rather than on mere driving force, officers will do the same thing. Captain Halahan, commanding the naval storming forces, who had repeatedly told me this was to be his last fight, was shot down and killed at the outset. Commander Edwards, standing near him on the gangway deck, was also shot down and completely incapacitated. Colonel Elliot, commanding the Marine storming forces, and his second-in-command, Major Cordner, were killed on the bridge, where they had taken up a commanding position in full view of the gangway deck. Many others were killed or wounded. The death of so many brave men was a terrible blow. Nobody knew better than they the tremendous risk attached to their actions – the pity of it was that they should not have lived to see the success for which they were so largely responsible.

At one minute past midnight the ship actually arrived alongside the Mole, one minute late on schedule time, having steamed alongside at 16 knots speed. The engines were immediately reversed at full speed and the ship bumped the Mole very gently on the specially constructed fender fitted on the port bow.

The conning position in the flame-thrower hut was well chosen, our heads being about 5 feet above the top of the Mole wall. We had previously devoted many hours to studying photographs of the Mole with the idea of recognising objects thereon. Our aerial confrères had photographed every portion of the Mole from almost every conceivable angle with both ordinary and stereoscopic cameras. We had also had picture postcards and other illustrations at our disposal. Though none of us had ever actually seen the Mole itself, we felt pretty sure of being able to recognise any portion of it immediately. In that we were over-confident. The smoke, the intermittent glare and flashes, the alternating darkness and the unceasing rain, added to the disturbance of one's attention caused by the noise and the explosion of shell, rendered observation somewhat difficult. As far as we could see we were to the westward of our desired position. The engines were, therefore, kept at full speed astern, and the ship, aided by a 3-knot tide running to the eastward, rapidly drifted in that direction. When sufficient sternway had been gathered the engines were put to full speed ahead to check her. A low building was then observed on the Mole abreast the ship, but it was not recognised immediately as the north-eastern shed (No. 3), which we had expected to appear much larger. The distance in the uncertain light was also very deceptive, the building in question appearing to be situated within a few feet of the outer wall, whereas it must have been at least 45 yards away.

But time was pressing. Our main diversion had certainly commenced, but at all costs we must have it fully developed before the blockships arrived at twenty minutes past midnight. The order was therefore given to let go the starboard anchor. A voice tube for this purpose led from the flame-thrower hut to the cable deck. The order was certainly not given *sotto voce*. But the noise at this time was terrific. I could not be certain whether the order was received as no answer was heard in reply. Certainly the anchor was not let go. Meanwhile the engines were ordered at full speed astern and full speed ahead alternately to keep the ship in position; the manner in which these orders were carried out by the engine-room staff, under the command of Engineering Lieutenant-Commander Bury, was admirable. No reply being forthcoming to questions as to the delay in anchoring, Rosoman left the conning tower and went below to investigate. The din had now reached a crescendo. Every gun that would bear appeared to be focused on our upper works. which were being hit every few seconds. Our guns in the fighting-top were pouring out a continuous hail of fire in reply. One could aptly say that we could hardly hear ourselves think.

At last I had news from the cable deck – this was a great relief, as I feared that the two heavy shells which burst between decks had killed all the anchoring party. The starboard anchor had jammed somewhere. It had been previously lowered to the water's edge and nothing was holding the cable, but it refused to budge. The port anchor was, therefore, dropped at the foot of the wall, and the ship allowed to drop astern until 100 yards of cable had been veered. The cable was then secured.

The ship immediately swung bodily out from the Mole. With the helm to starboard she swung in again, but with her bows so tight against the Mole, and her stern so far out, that the foremost gangways just failed to reach the top of the wall. With the helm amidships the ship lay parallel to the wall, but no gangways would reach. With the helm to port the ship again swung away from the Mole. This was an exceedingly trying situation. Everything now depended upon the *Daffodil* (Lieutenant H.G. Campbell).

It will be remembered that as a result of the towing hawser having parted, and in consequence of our increase of speed when running alongside, the *Iris* and the *Daffodil* had been left behind. We knew that whatever happened we could absolutely depend on Gibbs (Commander Valentine F. Gibbs had both legs shot away and died the next day) and Campbell making short work of any surmountable difficulty, and our trust was not misplaced. They must have cut off a considerable corner to have arrived as early as they did. The *Iris* steamed past us at her utmost speed, which was very slow, and went alongside the Mole about 100 yards ahead of *Vindictive* exactly as laid down in the Plan. Of her more anon.

After we had been struggling against our difficulties alongside for about five minutes *Daffodil* suddenly appeared steaming straight for our foremast in a direction perpendicular to the Mole. Campbell pushed her nose against us, hawsers were passed to his vessel, and he shoved us bodily alongside the Mole, exactly in accordance with the Plan. Really he might have been an old stager at tugmaster's work, pursuing his vocation in one of our own harbours, judging by the cool manner in which he carried out his instructions to the letter.

Immediately the two foremost gangways reached the wall they were lowered until they rested on it. No other gangways were then available. The order was at once passed to 'Storm the Mole.'

Owing to the light wind of the preceding day we had not expected to find any swell against the wall. The scend (upward surge in a heavy sea – Ed.) of the sea, however, was so heavy and so confused, as each wave rebounded, that the ship was rolling considerably. Every time she rolled over to port there was a heavy jarring bump which was probably caused by the bilge on the port side of the ship crashing down on the step of the Mole some few feet below the surface. The whole ship was shaking violently at each bump, and rolling so heavily that we were greatly apprehensive of sustaining vital damage below the water-line.

The Stokes gun batteries had already been bombing the Mole abreast the ship. The flame-throwers should also have helped to clear the way for the storming parties. The order had been given to switch on the foremost flame-thrower. Unfortunately the pipe leading from the containers to the hut had been severed somewhere below by a shell explosion. This was not noticed before the order was obeyed, with the result that many gallons of highly inflammable oil were squirted over the decks. One hesitates to think what would have happened if this oil had become ignited.

Incidentally, the actual nozzle of this flame-thrower was shot away just after the order to switch on had been given by the officer in charge, Lieutenant A.L. Eastlake, attached RE, who held the proud position of being the sole representative of the military on board the attacking vessels. Eastlake was the only other occupant of the hut, and I don't think he will easily forget the brief period that we experienced in that decidedly uncomfortable erection. Sparks were flying about inside, but somehow, at the time, one didn't connect the pyrotechnic display with the fact that they emanated from the medley of missiles passing through it. Curiously enough neither of us were hit, but our clothing sadly needed repair – an experience which was common enough in shore fighting, but unusual afloat where the missiles are generally rather too large to pass through one's headgear without removing one's head *en route*.

The other flame-thrower fared no better. Commander Brock was in charge. He lit the ignition apparatus and passed down the order to 'switch on.' The whole outfit of oil ran its course, but unfortunately, at the very commencement, the ignition apparatus was shot away, with the result that the instrument was converted into an oil thrower instead of emitting a flame.

Lieutenant-Commander B.F. Adams, leading a party of seamen, stormed the Mole immediately the gangways were placed. The only two gangways which could reach the Mole were, to say the least of it, very unsteady platforms. Their inboard ends were rising and falling several feet as the ship rolled; the outer ends were see-sawing and sliding backwards and forwards on the top of the Wall. My own personal impression at the time was that these gangways were alternately lifting off and resting on the wall, but apparently that was not so. The fact remains, however, that the run across these narrow gangways with a 30 foot drop beneath to certain death was not altogether inviting.

The first act of the advance party, in accordance with the instructions was to secure the ship to the wall by means of the grappling anchors. A great struggle to do this was undertaken. The foremost grappling anchors only just reached the Mole. Some men sat on the top of the wall and endeavoured to pull the grapnels over the top as they were lowered from the ship. These grapnels, by virtue of the use for which they were designed, were heavy. That fact, combined with the continuous rolling of the ship, made it exceedingly difficult to control them. Rosoman and a party of men on board joined in the struggle, but a heavy lurch of the ship broke up the davit on which the foremost grappling iron was slung, and the latter fell between the ship and the wall.

Adams' party were followed out in great style by the remainder of the seamen storming parties fed by their surviving officers, and then by the Marines. I propose to tell later of what occurred on the Mole itself, in so far as I have been able to gather from the parties concerned.

As soon as it was clear that the grappling anchors had failed us owing to the heavy swell there was no other alternative than to order *Daffodil* to carry on pushing throughout the proceedings.

A curious incident which has never been explained occurred just previously. Some individual in *Vindictive* had hailed *Daffodil* and called to them to shove off. 'By whose orders?' came the response shouted by Campbell from *Daffodil's* bridge. 'Captain Halahan's orders,' was the reply. As a matter of fact, poor gallant Halahan had been killed some ten minutes earlier. 'I take my orders from Captain Carpenter,' shouted Campbell. 'He's dead,' was shouted back. 'I don't believe it,' responded Campbell, and incidentally he was right, though I haven't the faintest idea what he based his belief on. As Mark Twain would have said, 'The report of my death was much exaggerated.' The incident was certainly curious, but of course (this for the benefit of those who, during the war, saw spies and traitors at every corner) there can only be the explanation that some poor wounded fellow must have been delirious.

Campbell had been shot in the face, but such a trifle as that didn't appear to have worried him, and he continued to push the *Vindictive* alongside from the moment of his arrival until the whole hour and five minutes had elapsed before we left the Mole. Originally the *Daffodil* had been detailed to secure alongside *Vindictive* as soon as the latter was secured to the Mole and then to disembark her demolition parties for their work on the Mole. That part of the plan could not be carried out, however, though several of his parties climbed over her bows into *Vindictive* on their way to accomplish it.

The demolition charges had been stowed outside the conning tower ready for use; on the passage across we had come to the conclusion that this was a case of risking the success of the whole landing for the furtherance of a secondary object, and the charges had therefore been removed to a safer position. This change of arrangement was indeed fortunate, for the deck on both sides of the conning tower became a regular shambles during the final approach. Yeoman of signals, John Buckley, who had volunteered to take up a position outside the conning tower in readiness to fire illuminating rockets, had remained at his post until killed. We found him there at the foot of his rocket tube in the morning, a splendid fellow who had been as helpful in the work of preparation as he was unflinching in the face of almost certain death. All the signal men except one had been either killed or completely disabled, and almost every soul on the conning tower platform had made the supreme sacrifice.

On the order being given to storm the Mole the storming parties had rushed up every available ladder to the gangway deck. At the top of the foremost ladder the men, in their eagerness to get at the enemy, were stumbling over a body. I had bent down to drag it clear, when one of the men shouted: 'That's Mr Walker, sir, he's had his arm shot off!' Immediately Walker, who was still conscious, heard this he waved his remaining hand to me and wished me the best of luck. This officer, Lieutenant H.T.C. Walker, survived.

The high wall, towering above our upper deck, was now protecting the hull of the ship from gun-fire; no vital damage could be sustained in that way so long as we remained alongside. The chief source of danger from which vital damage might come before we had completed our work at the Mole was that of the fast German motor boats stationed at Blankenberge. The latter harbour was barely five minutes' steaming distance away, and, as the enemy would now be fully cognisant of our position, we might reasonably expect a horde of these craft to come to the attack with torpedos. It does not require much naval knowledge to realise that the difficulty of avoiding torpedo fire under such circumstances would be well-nigh insuperable. Where a torpedo craft of that description can suddenly rush in from the outer darkness a large vessel has to depend upon remaining unseen; but, of course, such tactics were now impossible, and, still further, a torpedo could not be avoided even if seen coming towards the ship. That we were not attacked in that manner was mainly due to the work of certain of our smaller craft specially detailed to deal with the Blankenberge force; former experience of the latter also led us to believe that the German personnel in those boats had no stomach for a fight.

Our guns in the fighting-top were directing a murderous heavy gun battery at the end of the broad part of the Mole, and the lighter battery on the lighthouse extension. In neither case could the enemy's guns bear on the ship, and we had the advantage of taking the former battery from the rear and giving the latter a taste of enfilading fire from its western flank. But there was another target of importance. Immediately abreast the ship a German destroyer was berthed alongside the inner wharf of the Mole only 80 yards distant from the ship. We had an uninterrupted view of the greater part of her between the two northern sheds, her bridges showing well above the ground level of the Mole. Our guns in the fighting-top, in charge of Lieutenant Charles N.B. Rigby, RMA, riddled that destroyer through and through. We could see the projectiles hitting the Mole floor whenever the gun was temporarily depressed, and then shower upon shower of sparks as they tore through the destroyer's upperworks. The vessel appeared to have sunk, as very little of her upper deck could be seen, although we had such an elevated viewpoint, but now I think it possible that the wall protected her vitals, and that she escaped complete destruction from our gun-fire.

There seems little doubt that our fighting-top was now coming in for the attention of most of the enemy guns. Presently a tremendous crash overhead, followed by a cessation of our fire, indicated that a heavy shell had made havoc with poor Rigby and his crew of eight men. As a matter of fact, that shell had wrecked the whole fighting-top, killed all the personnel except three gunners who were all severely wounded, and dismounted one of the guns. The only survivor who was not completely disabled – Sergeant Finch, RMA, struggled out from the shambles somehow and, without a thought for his own wounds, examined the remaining gun, found it was still intact, and continued to fight single-handed. Another survivor, Gunner Sutton, who had again been wounded, fired the remaining ammunition when Finch could no longer carry on; finally, a German shell completely destroyed the remains of this gun position. The splendid work of Lieutenant Rigby and his guns' crews had been invaluable, and one cannot but attribute the complete success of our diversion very largely to these gallant men. Rigby himself had set a wonderful example; all who knew him had never doubted that he would so do. Finch survived and was afterwards voted the Victoria Cross by the men of the Royal Marines.

As soon as the ship had been securely anchored the howitzer guns manned by the RMA in charge of Captain Reginald Dallas-Brookes, RMA, commenced to bombard the targets specially assigned to them. The German batteries on the mainland were shelling our position at the Mole for all they were worth, but their efforts must have been hampered by the continuous fire of our howitzers. The presence of such weapons on board ship was, to say the least of it, most unusual. *Vindictive*'s nature had undergone an unusual change as soon as she was secured to the Mole. The direction and range of the enemy's batteries had been worked out beforehand for any position alongside the wall. We were, therefore, in the novel situation of being able to drop heavy howitzer shells upon the enemy's batteries less than a mile away, a decided change from ordinary battleship target practice where ranges of 10–15 miles were the order of the day.

The 7.5-inch howitzer gun on the forecastle could not be used. A heavy shell had burst amongst the original gun's crew and had killed or disabled them all. A second crew was sent from one of the naval 6-inch guns in the battery and was just being detailed to work the howitzer when another shell killed, or disabled, all but two men. Soon after opening fire the midship 7.5-inch howitzer was damaged by another shell which killed some of the crew, but the remainder repaired the gun under great difficulty and managed to resume the firing later on. The 11-inch howitzer on the quarter-deck was extremely well handled. This gun fired at a steady rate throughout the proceedings in spite of the darkness, the fumes, the difficulty of man-handling such large projectiles in a cramped-up space and the battering that the ship was receiving around them. The behaviour of the RMA throughout was fine; they worked with a will which may have been equalled elsewhere, but which has certainly never been surpassed; the example set by Captain Brooks was altogether splendid.

Mention must be made of the pyrotechnic party as we called them. Having located and reached the Mole ourselves an early duty was that of indicating its extremity to the approaching blockships. For this purpose a rocket station was rigged up in my cabin below. The rocket apparatus protruded through a port in the stern of the ship and had been placed at an angle calculated to carry the rocket behind the lighthouse before bursting, so that the lighthouse would show clearly against an illuminated background. One of the party was told off for this position, instructed as to the object to be attained, and ordered to carry on according to his own judgment. I believe this man had never previously served afloat and had never been in action, but, like the rest of them, he did his bit without the slightest hesitation and, judging by results, with 100 per cent. efficiency. Others of the pyrotechnic brigade landed with the storming parties and worked portable flame-throwers, special flares, etc., before finally attending the smoke-making apparatus and assisting with the wounded. Lieutenant Graham S. Hewett, RNVR, was in command of the pyrotechnic party.

A few minutes after the storming of the Mole had commenced a terrific explosion was seen away to the westward, and we guessed that the submarine party had attacked the viaduct. A seaman was standing near me at the time and brought back to me an old remark of mine when he asked, 'Was that it, sir?' The explosion presented a wonderful spectacle. The flames shot up to a great height – one mentally considered it at least a mile. Curiously enough the noise of the explosion was not heard. The experiences of the submarines will be related presently.

At about 12.15am the blockships were expected to be close to the Mole, and a momentary glimpse of them was obtained as they passed close to the lighthouse on their way to the canal entrance. So far so good. We saw nothing more of the blockships and received no further news of them until the operation had been completed. Nevertheless, no news was good news under the circumstances and we felt quite confident that the blockships had not been seriously hampered by the German Mole defences. Our primary object was, therefore, attained; the diversion had been of sufficient magnitude.

Our further tasks were firstly that of continuing the diversion until the crews of the blockships had had a reasonable chance of being rescued subsequent to sinking their vessels in the canal, secondly of re-embarking our storming parties and withdrawing to seaward, and thirdly of carrying out demolition work on the Mole during our stay alongside. It will be noticed that these three tasks are not mentioned in their proper sequence of event but in their order of importance. It is obviously true that demolition work might be of assistance from the point of view of diversion, but not to a great extent when one realises that the enemy were already so animated with a desire to destroy our ship that they would hardly care one way or the other what our particular action on the Mole might be. The presence of the ship was the main diversion and so, at all costs, the ship must be kept alongside until the diversion was no longer required and until our storming parties had returned.

At about half an hour after midnight the full force of the diversion had been developed. Although the ship was still being hit continuously and the inferno showed no signs of abatement one can say that the conditions had become stabilised. As far as we could gather we could not augment our efforts, but could only carry on for the time being. So we carried on.

Being somewhat anxious as to the state of things between decks I took the opportunity of a hurried visit below. On my way down from the bridge I met Lieutenant E. Hilton-Young, RNVR, our parliamentary representative. He was attired in his shirt sleeves and minus any head-gear. His right arm was bandaged. I remember that he was breaking all the accepted rules of the drill-book by smoking a large cigar as he performed his prearranged duties of supervising the foremost 6-inch guns and his self-appointed duty of cheering everybody up. On inquiry he informed me that he had 'got one in the arm.' I heard afterwards that even when he had collapsed he refused to have his wound attended to, and had to be taken below by force. Eventually his right arm had to be amputated, but with his unfailing resource he didn't let many hours pass by before commencing to educate himself in the art of left-handed writing.

Every available space on the mess deck was occupied by casualties. Those who could do so were sitting on the mess stools awaiting their turn for medical attention. Many were stretched at full length on the deck, the majority being severely wounded. Some had already collapsed and were in a state of coma; I fear that many had already passed away. It was a sad spectacle indeed. Somehow, amidst all the crashing and smashing on deck, one had not realised the sacrifice that was taking place.

During a fight at sea the personnel below know little or nothing of how things are going. This especially applies to the stokehold and engine-room personnel, who are in an unenviable position. It applies, also, to the wounded who have been carried below. It is not difficult to imagine their feelings, especially when one considers how rapidly a vessel may sink after sustaining a vital injury. One does not need to be an advanced psychologist to understand the importance of keeping those stationed between decks supplied with information as to what is occurring on deck. So I shouted out something about everything going splendidly, the Mole being stormed, the viaduct being blown up and the blockships having passed in. The cheer that went up will live long in my memory. Those who could stand crowded round and forgot their wounds. Some of those on the deck endeavoured to sit up to ascertain the news. I did not then know that I had been reported as killed. The crowd almost barred my way in and the question which caught my ear more than any other was, 'Have we won, sir, have we won?' just as if the whole affair had been a football match.

The medical officers and their assistants, under the direction of Staff-Surgeon McCutcheon, were working at the highest pressure. The wounded were literally pouring down every available ladder in a constant stream. Dressing stations had been improvised at intervals along the deck, the ward-room and the sick bay being the two main stations. Everything humanly possible was being done to render first-aid and to alleviate suffering. There was no lack of ready helpers. All those of the latter who could do so were bringing the wounded down. Many of the less severely wounded were attending to those others who were badly hit. A Marine with his own head bandaged up was supporting in his arms an officer who was unconscious with a terrible wound in the head, and only relaxed his hold when the officer died. The work of McCutcheon and his confréres (the other medical staff) was beyond all praise; untiring energy, consummate care, and withal real brotherly bearing characterised their actions.

The news of the blockships spread quickly, and one heard every now and then renewed outbursts of cheering. The news had reached the stokehold and did much to relieve the tension amongst the personnel in that part of the ship. A few pieces of shell had fallen into the engine room, but no damage had been done.

A return to the lower bridge showed little apparent change in the situation. Shell were still hitting us every few seconds and many casualties were being caused by flying splinters. Large pieces of the funnels and ventilators were being torn out and hurled in all directions – one wondered how much more of this battering the ship could stand. The exact nature of the various missiles and the direction from whence they came were of course unknown to us. It was afterwards suggested that the shore guns to the westward of Blankenberge were doing much of the mischief. Certainly our position, tangential to the Mole, brought such a thing into the realm of possibility, but it would seem doubtful whether those German batteries, from which we were probably invisible, would risk hitting their own guns on the Mole from that flanking direction. However, all our guns which could fire at the enemy were fully occupied in accordance with the prearranged plan, so there was no particular object in ascertaining the position of new targets.

Our chief anxiety at this period was the safety of *Daffodil*, which seemed to bear a charmed life. *Vindictive*'s hull was amptly protected by the wall itself, but *Daffodil* was far more exposed. As already mentioned the loss of *Daffodil* would almost certainly have entailed the loss of the whole of the storming parties on the Mole.

IV

As soon as the two foremost gangways reached the wall a party of seamen led by Lieutenant-Commander Adams had commenced the storming of the Mole. Lieutenant-Commander A.L. Harrison, the senior officer of the seamen storming parties, had been wounded in the head and was too dazed to land on the Mole until later. Commander Brock, having completed his duties in the aft flame-thrower hut, also stormed the Mole.

Adams and a handful of men made their way along the parapet to the left and found an observation hut situated on it close by. This was bombed, but no occupants were found inside. Brock is believed to have gone inside this hut for the purpose of examining its interior; there is no authentic evidence that he was ever seen again. Adams stationed some of his men to guard a ladder leading from the parapet to the floor of the Mole and then returned to find us struggling with the grappling anchors as already described. Adams then reconnoitred again to the eastward and located a German machine gun firing at the parapet from the trench system on the floor of the Mole. Barbed wire surrounded this trench, which interposed between *Vindictive* and the three-gun battery at the end of the broad part of the Mole. The seamen were then detailed to bomb the trench position, but in doing so they suffered many casualties from machine-gun fire. The position on the parapet was almost entirely exposed to gun-fire from the Mole itself, the look-out station affording the only cover. The German vessels berthed at the inner side of the Mole had also joined in the fight.

The terrific noise, the darkness, the bursting of shell and the hail of machine-gun bullets rendered it exceedingly difficult for any one individual to make such observations as would lead to a connected account of the fighting on the Mole itself.

Just before arriving alongside the Mole, Lieutenant-Commander Harrison, in supreme command of the seamen storming parties after Captain Halahan's death, was struck on the head by a fragment of a shell; he was knocked senseless and sustained a broken jaw. On recovering consciousness he proceeded over one of the gangways to the parapet, where he took over command of the party detailed to attack the Mole batteries to the eastward, Lieutenant-Commander Adams going back to obtain reinforcements. Gathering together a handful of his men, Harrison led a charge along the parapet itself in the face of heavy machine gun tire. He was killed at the head of his men, all but two of whom were also killed, these two being wounded.

Harrison's charge down that narrow gangway of death was a worthy finale to the large number of charges which, as a forward of the first rank, he had led down many a Rugby football ground. He had 'played the game' to the end. To quote the final words in the official notification of his posthumous award of the Victoria Cross: 'Lieutenant-Commander Harrison, although already severely wounded and undoubtedly in great pain, displayed indomitable resolution and courage of the highest order in pressing his attack, knowing as he did that any delay in silencing the guns might jeopardise the main object of the expedition, i.e. the blocking of the Zeebrugge-Bruges Canal.'

With Harrison's death the Navy lost an officer who was as popular and as keen as he had been invaluable to the success of this particular operation, especially in the preparatory work. Able-seaman McKenzie, one of the survivors of Harrison's party, finding himself alone, did good execution with his Lewis gun in spite of being wounded in several places; he eventually returned to *Vindictive* after accounting for a number of the enemy.

The Marines, now commanded by Major B.G. Weller, RMLI, had followed the seamen over the gangways. The prearranged details of the operations on the Mole had to be somewhat modified owing to the fact that *Vindictive* was further to the westward than originally intended. The reason for the latter has already been given, but a further word may not be out of place. The responsibility for the actual position of the ship was entirely my own; the error in position was, therefore, my own also. When the attack was originally planned the intention had been to endeavour to place the ship with her stern 70 yards from the western gun of the battery on the lighthouse extension. Actually *Vindictive*'s gangways rested on the Mole nearly 300 yards to the westward. One can only conjecture what would have happened, under the circumstances of the failure of the smoke screen owing to the change of wind, if the ship had proceeded past the six-gun battery at a speed sufficiently slow for berthing so close to the battery itself. Whether the ship would ever have reached the Mole, or whether there would have been any storming parties left on arrival alongside, can only be guessed. It certainly looks as if our mistake in position was as providential as it was unintentional.

Lieutenant F.T.V. Cooke, who afterwards greatly distinguished himself, led out the first party of Marines and silenced a party of Germans who were observed firing at the parapet from a position near No. 2 shed. Another party, under Lieutenant Lamplough, then established a strong point near No. 3 shed for the purpose of dealing with any enemy approaching from the westward. His party also attacked and bombed a German destroyer berthed at the inner side of the Mole.

Another party was ordered to the eastward to reinforce the seamen. As soon as the position was more clear the main party of the Marine force, under Captain E. Bamford, commenced an assault on the German positions covering the Mole battery.

It is not possible to say how many of the storming parties reached the Mole, the loss of officers and men and the resulting temporary disorganisation naturally prevented the collection of definite information. Suffice it to say that a large number stormed the Mole in furtherance of our diversion, and that the latter was undoubtedly successful in that we attained our primary object of assisting the blockships to pass an all-important obstacle in the Mole batteries.

Before passing on to other phases of the operation a general idea of the difficulties faced by the storming parties may be of interest, together with a brief account of the manner in which these difficulties were surmounted.

From the time of our arrival the Mole abreast the ship was subjected to extremely heavy fire. Presumably the shore guns, including the Kaiser Wilhelm battery with its 12-inch guns and the Goeben battery (9.4-inch guns) situated almost within point-blank range, were shelling the Mole for all they were worth, regardless of damage to their own property or of danger to their own personnel. That, of course, would be a correct action, the repulse of the enemy always being of first importance.

The parapet on the high wall was almost entirely destitute of cover. The difficulty of placing the scaling ladders from the parapet to the floor-level of the Mole and of descending them whilst carrying such paraphernalia as rifles, bombs, flame throwers, Lewis guns, etc., can easily be imagined. The difficulty would certainly not be lessened by the fact that the men would have their backs to any enemy who might be awaiting them on the Mole itself. The fighting amidst entirely strange surroundings in the face of properly organised strong-points held by the enemy would not be easy. Add to that the certain losses and consequent disorganisation entailed during the assault, the difficulty of recognising friend from foe at night, and the blinding glare of star shell or searchlights alternating with momentary periods of inky darkness.

Undoubtedly the assault would be difficult enough. But what of the retirement? The bodies of any men who were killed or disabled on the Mole could only be re-embarked by way of the vertical ladders against the wall. It would be bad enough to descend them in the first place, but a herculean task to carry a body 20 feet up a vertical ladder under incessant shell and machine-gun fire. Yet, and I think this fact sums up the splendid gallantry of these men, of the large number of men who stormed the Mole, many of whom were killed or completely disabled, the total number left on the Mole after the retirement, including both dead and wounded, amounted to little more than a dozen.

Daffodil, as already described, was prevented from landing her demolition parties in the prearranged manner, but some of them, led by Sub-Lieutenant F.E. Chevallier, had climbed into *Vindictive* and made their way to the Mole. Lieutenant C.C. Dickinson, commanding the demolition parties, and a party of his men on board *Vindictive* had landed at the commencement of the assault. They placed a couple of ladders, descended them and then proceeded across the Mole, killing some Germans who were apparently making for the ladders. Demolition charges were placed in position, but not actually exploded owing to the presence of our own men in the vicinity. There is little doubt that the demolition parties would have been able to carry out considerable destructive work if more time had been available. Whatever the results of their efforts it is certain that Dickinson, Chevallier, and their men did all that was possible under the circumstances.

Iris had reached the Mole and dropped her anchor at the foot of the wall, about 12.15am, her position being roughly 100 yards ahead, i.e., to the westward, of *Vindictive*. The heavy swell was tossing her about like a cork, with the result that the use of the parapet anchors was extremely difficult. After several failures to get these parapet anchors hooked to the top of the wall Lieutenant Claude E.K. Hawkings, one of the officers of the storming party, ordered some men to hold up one of the scaling ladders. They could not actually lean it against the wall; the rough nature of the latter and the surging of the ship would have combined to break the ladder immediately. The ladder was, therefore, merely sloping towards the wall without any support at its upper end. Hawkings ran up it and leaped to the top of the Mole, the ladder being smashed to pieces a moment later. He sat astride the wall for the purpose of fixing an anchor and appears to have been immediately attacked by some enemy on the parapet itself. He was seen defending himself with his revolver before he was actually killed. It was terribly sad that this great act should have cost him his life.

Lieutenant-Commander George N. Bradford, who was actually in command of the storming party in *Iris* and whose duties did not include that of securing the ship, climbed up the ship's derrick which carried a large parapet anchor and which was rigged out over the Mole side of the ship. The derrick itself was crashing on the Mole with each movement of the ship, which, in turn, was rolling and pitching heavily; a more perilous climb can scarcely be imagined. Waiting his opportunity Bradford chose the right moment and jumped to the wall, taking the anchor with him. He placed the latter in position, but almost immediately was riddled with machine-gun bullets and fell into the sea between *Iris* and the Mole. Gallant attempts were made to rescue his body, but owing to the darkness and the rush of the strong tidal stream he was swept away beyond recovery.

Nothing could have been finer than Bradford's efforts to secure the ship. He had been a splendid fighter in the 'ring'; it was against his nature to give in as long as there was the remotest chance of winning through; his death brought us a great loss of a great gentleman. Really, one cannot conceive greater bravery than was shown by these two officers, who have set an example which will surely never be forgotten.

The anchor placed by Bradford had either slipped or been shot away, with the result that *Iris* suddenly surged out from the Mole. It was then obvious that the difficulty of securing to the Mole was insuperable, so Commander Gibbs very rightly decided to land his men across *Vindictive*. He therefore ordered the cable to be slipped and then steamed round the stern of *Daffodil* and came alongside *Vindictive*. This change of plan, necessitated by the unfavourable state of the sea, showed a highly credible degree of initiative. It must be realised that these movements and proceedings of *Iris* had occupied over half an hour; it was about 12.55am before *Iris* was secured to *Vindictive*. By that time the order for the retirement had been given. A few men scrambled out of *Iris*, but that ship was almost immediately ordered to shove off. She therefore left *Vindictive* and shaped course to the northward. She had barely turned when she came under a heavy fire from some enemy batteries. Two large shell and several small shell hit her, and were closely followed by three more large shell. The look-out house at the port extremity of the bridge was destroyed and a serious fire was caused on the upper deck.

Valentine Gibbs, who had remained on the bridge throughout the operation, was mortally wounded. I had known 'Val', as we had always called him, since he was a boy of thirteen. Even at that age he had shown himself to be absolutely fearless. Later in life he had risen rapidly in his profession and would assuredly have been marked out for high command in due course. In peace days he had won the great race on the Cresta Run at St Moritz; in war he had volunteered for every dangerous operation for which he had the remotest chance of selection. At last his opportunity had come and he lived for nought else than to put *Iris* alongside Zeebrugge Mole. I was told afterwards that in his short periods of consciousness after being wounded he asked and repeated but one question, 'How are things going?' and he continued to ask how things were going until he died. I cannot write more of 'Val', words and phrases fail to do him justice.

The havoc in *Iris* was serious. From *Vindictive* she appeared to have been sunk, for she suddenly disappeared in a cloud of smoke and flame.

Major C.E.E. Eagles, DSO, in command of the Marine storming parties in *Iris*, was killed, and many of his men were killed and wounded at this period. Artificial smoke was emitted and a small motor boat also laid a smoke screen to shoreward of *Iris* – this probably accounted for her sudden disappearance from view.

The navigating officer had been seriously wounded. Lieutenant Oscar Henderson took command. Petty Officer Smith was illuminating the compass with a torch in one hand and steering with the other. Able-Seaman F.E. Blake, having extinguished the fire on the bridge, employed himself in throwing overboard live bombs which were lying amongst the burning debris on the upper deck.

Iris had not received her share of good fortune. Nevertheless, although she actually failed to land her storming parties, there is every probability that her proceedings assisted to enhance the success of the diversion at the Mole and thereby materially assisted towards the safe passage of the blockships, i.e., the attainment of our object.

V

I previously mentioned that the explosion of the submarine took place shortly after the storming of the Mole had commenced. The immediate purpose in destroying the railway viaduct connecting the Mole to the mainland was twofold: firstly, that of preventing the Germans from sending reinforcements across to the help of the Mole garrison; secondly, that of augmenting the main diversion. There were, however, ulterior objects also. Firstly, the destruction in itself would be a valuable art of the general work of demolition designed to reduce the efficiency of the Mole as a naval and aerial base; secondly, the loss of the railway would deny to the enemy the use of the Mole as a place of embarkation for military purposes. If deprived of railway communication the Mole would lose a high percentage of its special war value.

Two old submarines, *C1*, commanded by Lieutenant Aubrey C. Newbold, and *C3*, commanded by Lieutenant Richard D. Sandford, were chosen for the purpose – each carrying a volunteer crew of one officer and four men in addition to the officer in command.

The submarines were provided with special control apparatus so that the personnel, after having set the apparatus to guide the vessel to its destination, could abandon their craft before reaching the viaduct itself.

For the purpose of abandonment each submarine was given motor-driven skiffs and special ladders. The latter might enable the crews to climb up the viaduct and escape before the explosion took place, the motor-skiffs being supplied for escaping to seaward if that was found to be feasible.

Each submarine carried a heavy cargo of high explosive. This latter was fitted with time fuses and special instruments so that there would be sufficient delay between the ignition of the fuse and the final explosion. At a prearranged minute after passing position G, the submarines were to have slipped from their towing hawsers and then to have made the best of their way to the viaduct. Unfortunately *C1* was so much delayed by the parting of a hawser that she could not continue her voyage to the viaduct without running the risk of hampering *C3*. The latter, exactly in accordance with the Plan, slipped from tow and proceeded under her own engines on the prearranged courses. At midnight the submarine appears to have been sighted in the light of a star shell. Searchlights immediately picked her up and some firing was seen in their direction. Artificial smoke was immediately made use of, but the wind, having then commenced to blow towards the north, was found to be unfavourable. The firing was only of short duration and the artificial smoke was switched off. A few minutes later the viaduct showed up clearly against a glare in the background and course was altered to ensure striking exactly at right angles. Sandford disdained to use the control apparatus to take his submarine into her position.

The vessel was run under the viaduct, at a speed of nearly 10 knots, immediately between two of the vertical piles. She charged against the horizontal and diagonal girders with such force as to penetrate the framework of the viaduct as far as her own conning tower, whilst being lifted bodily about a couple of feet on the frames. Firmly wedged under the railway in a position about 50 yards from the northern end of the viaduct the first part of the operation was completed. It is difficult to account for the small opposition offered to her approach by the enemy. Possibly they mistook her for a friend. Another suggestion is that they thought she was endeavouring to pass under the viaduct en route to the canal, and, knowing this was impossible, that they hoped to capture her intact. That suggestion sounds extremely unlikely. Possibly the diversion caused by our efforts at the other end of the Mole had distracted the attention of the defence commanders; the men may have feared to take unexpected measures on their own responsibility. Whatever the reason for the lack of enemy opposition there was certainly no lack of difficulty. The darkness, suddenly giving way to the blinding glare of searchlights, the navigational difficulties, and the necessary care in handling such an awkward vessel combined to make their arrival a very fine feat. But finer was to follow.

Several of the enemy had appeared on the viaduct and commenced to fire on her with machine guns from close range; the latter cannot have amounted to many feet! The crew lowered a motor skiff and Sandford ordered them to abandon ship. He then fired the time fuse and jumped into the boat. Their purpose was now to steam away to the westward at utmost speed so as to get well clear before the explosion took place. Unfortunately the skiff's engine was useless – the propeller had been broken! Oars had been provided for such emergency and the crew pulled away from the viaduct for dear life. As soon as the boat was clear of the viaduct itself the firing became intense, both from the viaduct and from the shore. The German searchlights were directed on to the boat.

Many miracles occurred that night, but none more extraordinary than the escape of this little boat with its two officers and four men. Presently Sandford himself and his Petty Officer were severely wounded; the stoker was also wounded. The boat was hit again and again, but fortunately the motor pump was working and the water could be rapidly ejected. Sandford was again wounded.

The skiff had managed to struggle about 300 yards from the viaduct when there was a deafening roar as submarine C3, the viaduct above her, the railway on the viaduct, and the Germans on the railway were hurled to destruction. It must have been a wonderful moment for Sandford and his crew.

The enemy searchlights were immediately extinguished and the firing died away. A few minutes later a picket boat – the ordinary type of steamboat carried by all large men-of-war – emerged from the darkness and hailed the skiff. The occupants of the latter were assisted into the picket boat, which then proceeded seawards and placed them on board the destroyer *Phoebe*.

The picket boat, under the charge of Lieutenant-Commander F.H. Sandford, RN, brother of the commander of the submarine, had been detailed for this rescue work. She had made a great part of the overseas journey under her own steam and had arrived in the nick of time to effect the rescue. Sandford, the Lieutenant-Commander, had been largely responsible for working out the details of the attack on the viaduct in addition to the preparations for the demolition work on the Mole. His handling of the picket boat – incidentally she returned the whole way home again under her own steam – was excellent.

Submarine *C1* saw what was probably the glare of the explosion caused by *C3*, but could not be certain whether the latter had reached her destination or not. They therefore waited until they considered ample time had passed for *C3* to have arrived at the viaduct if all had gone well. *C1* then approached the Mole en route towards the viaduct and sighted *Vindictive* retiring to the northward. This appeared to signify that the forces were retiring and that the operation had either been completed or had been found impracticable owing to the change of wind. Lieutenant Newbold, therefore, had to decide as to whether he should continue for the sake of augmenting the destruction caused by *C3* or whether he should haul off so as to be available for any further services required. It was a difficult decision to make. He chose the latter and earned the Vice-Admiral's commendation for doing so.

Those of us who were *au fait* with the details of the operation little thought we should ever see these heroic attackers of the viaduct again. The chances against manoeuvring a submarine into the viaduct were very considerable, the chances of any of the personnel being rescued were apparently nil. Nobody knew that better than the personnel concerned. The use of the control apparatus would have greatly increased their chances of being rescued, but they refused to consider preservation of life until the success of their undertaking had been assured. They cannot have expected to return. Yet there was no dearth of volunteers. The personnel had been selected in much the same way as those from the Grand Fleet. If the secret could have been made known beforehand and volunteers asked for in the ordinary way we should probably have had the whole submarine service begging to be allowed to take part.

The execution of this most difficult submarine operation was beyond all praise; it was, indeed, a miracle that the crew of C3 lived to witness the unqualified success of their efforts. Before the night was ended these gallant lives were again in jeopardy.

We heard afterwards that a German cyclist corps was hurriedly sent to reinforce the Mole garrison, and, not knowing that the viaduct had been destroyed, they were precipitated into the sea and thus infringed the Gadarene copyright (relating to or engaged in a headlong rush).

CHAPTER EIGHT

THE DAYLIGHT RAID

By MRS C.S. PEEL

The raid which made the most impression on Londoners was perhaps the daylight raid of 13 June 1917. A Special Constable says, 'I was returning to Walton Street after inspecting the Albert Hall patrol when I was told by a constable that a warning was out. I hurried home to warn my wife, who I found was just starting for the Ministry in which she worked. She decided to make a start, and I walked to the Oratory with her and saw her into an omnibus, as I thought it would turn out to be a dash raid by one or two planes and that she would hear the guns in plenty of time to take cover. It was before the days of maroon warnings. I walked as far as Yeomans Row (a turning out of Brompton Road) on my way to Walton Street Police Station, and as I passed the mews I saw a constable and asked if anything was on. "If you look over there you will see what's on," he replied, and on looking north-east over the houses I saw a cloud of aeroplanes. Then the guns began. I walked down Yeomans Row ordering the women and children into the houses, but on reaching the yard doors of the police station I looked round and saw they had all come out again, so I returned to repeat my orders. It was quite useless, come into the street they would. One woman, I recollect, stood with her baby in her arms pointing up, and saying, "Look at the airyplanes, Baby, look at the airyplanes." So I returned and stood in the yard and watched the airyplanes myself. There appeared to be about thirty huge black planes going very slowly, and a large number of much smaller planes flying very much faster. Some of these seemed to drop out of the clouds – evidently firing at the larger planes, which seemed to take no notice and continued in formation, led by one machine well ahead of the main body. Shells appeared to be bursting all round them as well as 2 or 3 miles away. The planes when I first saw them were, I think, heading directly for South Kensington via Piccadilly Circus, but when I was standing in the yard they seemed to turn south. I judged them to be over the city, and I put their height at about 5,000 feet. I believe actually it varied from 12,000 to 15,000, my mistake no doubt being due to the fact that they were the first twin-engine bombers I or anyone else had seen, and were twice as large as any we had used in this country at that time. I was rather alarmed at the idea of forty or fifty machines heading directly for our part of London, but the sight was so magnificent that I stood in the yard spellbound. The noise of the air being churned up by this fleet of aeroplanes was very loud.

'I was brought to my senses by a piece of shell whistling down close to me, so I took cover behind the wall of the Section House. I then watched the procession pass right across my front. An ambitious gunner somewhere in the district west of London thought he would have a few shots at them, but could only reach half-way and he burst one shell somewhere behind me and another over my head. Pieces came rattling down, one close to me in the yard, another on the front of the station buildings and a number in the Brompton Road. I bolted into the doorway of the Section House and stayed there for two or three minutes. My curiosity, however, overcame my funk, and I emerged again to see the cloud of planes turning away in a south-easterly direction. I counted twenty-five, but I fancy there were many more of ours which I could not see. The guns were still firing heavily, the big Hyde Park guns being particularly active. I was then instructed to go and see if No. 2 Patrol was all right. At the top of Yeomans Row I came across a laundry van, a woman holding the horse's head. She was very frightened, but sticking it out pluckily. A girl of about twenty-two was sitting inside crying. The woman told me that she had been in Knightsbridge, and the bombs had come down in quantities. I assured her no planes had passed over our end of London, but she said that the bombs had dropped – dozens of them – all round the Barracks. She had evidently mistaken the noise of the Hyde Park guns, which had been firing rapidly, for bombs. I began to feel extremely uneasy as to the safety of my wife.'

The wife in question may now take up the tale: 'I got into the omnibus at the Brompton Oratory, but as I was thinking about some work on which I was engaged I forgot about the raid warning. Often there were warnings and nothing more happened. Then suddenly it was borne in upon me that we were going very slowly and that the conductor was hanging on to the stairway rail and bending backwards staring into the sky, and that all the people on the pavement were staring too. One man walking head in air fell into the gutter. The omnibus was almost empty, so I joined the conductor and stared too. Up in the sky were numbers of aeroplanes. I thought, "Well, of course, those can't be enemy planes: they couldn't get here in broad daylight without any one shooting at them," so I went on staring. We were nearing the Knightsbridge stopping place, which in those days was opposite the Hyde Park Hotel. Then the guns began. The omnibus stopped and the conductor said, "You'd best take cover." Knowing that Hyde Park House was then used as a department of the Admiralty, I ran into it. There was no one in the hall, so I made for the stairs leading to the basement. By this time the noise was deafening, and I was convinced that bombs were falling. The basement was packed with women clerks, some of whom were crying hysterically. One caught hold of me. "Oh, I'm going to be killed! I'm going to be killed!" she moaned, pinching my arm so violently that what with pain and excitement I fired up and replied quite venomously, "I hope you *will*," which so surprised her that she stood still staring at me with her mouth open, the picture of idiocy. A girl near who also had been crying, but quietly, remarked, "You aren't very sympathetic." "I'm sorry," said I, beginning to recover my temper, "but my sympathies are with the men who have to bear this kind of thing day after day and night after night. So suppose you get some of these girls to be quiet." I wasn't in the least brave, but I *was* excited.

'After the guns ceased I nerved myself to go upstairs again, thinking that the street would be full of dead and dying people and that I must do what I could for them. What do you think I found? The whole place deserted except for a butcher's boy on a bicycle with a leg of mutton in his basket and a dreary-looking woman who had been selling flags and now began to try to sell them again. "Won't you buy a flag?" she asked me, in a voice which sounded as dreary as she looked, so I bought a flag, and as there were no cabs or omnibuses, or rather only a few driverless derelicts, I started to walk across the park to the Ministry. There all was in a turmoil, and the authorities decided that it would be wiser to dismiss the women for that day.

'Personally I think they were wrong, and that they should have required them to go on as usual, which with any encouragement they would have done. So I found myself with a spare afternoon, which had not happened to me for a very long time. I went to my club for luncheon and then played bridge. We had played several hands when suddenly I felt that I was going to faint, and in a wobbly voice and for no particular reason said, "No Trumps," laid down my cards and pinched myself as hard as I could, which was not as hard as that girl in Hyde Park House had pinched. By the time I recovered and again looked at my cards I was so alarmed at seeing the hand on which I had gone 'No Trumps' that I nearly fainted a second time. As I was coming home that evening in an omnibus it skidded violently, and to my horror I found myself saying, "Well, I can't bear this, it's too much," and began to cry.'

This story reminds one of the scene in the Gaiety Theatre when, owing to a bomb falling nearby, a quantity of dust and plaster fell on the audience. An officer home on leave was sitting in the stalls with a girl. She said that he clutched hold of her arm and as if hypnotised stared and stared at her. 'It's no business to happen here, you know,' he kept saying, 'it's no business to happen here.' She thought he had gone mad, and was so alarmed for him that she forgot to be frightened for herself. He explained to her afterwards that to be bombed in England seemed to 'destroy something in him.'

Every one talked about their daylight raid experiences. A girl who had come up to London the previous week was walking across Kensington Gardens that day. She heard the droning of aeroplanes and looked up to see a number of them flying in perfect formation. 'It never dawned on me that they were enemy planes and that I might be in danger,' she said. 'Then the battle began and I honestly confess I was terrified, although if one must be in a raid I suppose one could not have been in a safer place than the open park. A man in khaki was a few steps in front of me. The sight of his uniform steadied me. "I expect he often has to bear this kind of thing, poor dear!" I said to myself. "What do you think they are?" I called to him. "I don't know," he replied, "but they aren't ours, so I suppose they are German." I asked him if we could do anything to escape them. I felt sure they were all looking at me and would drop a bomb just for fun, on the chance of hitting me! "We can't do anything but lie down flat on the ground," he replied, "and they will be far away by the time we do that." So we continued to talk and watched them fly away.'

CHAPTER NINE

THE DEATH OF RICHTHOFEN

By 'Vigilant'

'It is impossible to fly across the Ancre in a westerly direction on account of strong enemy opposition. I must ask for this aerial barrage to be forced back, so that a reconnaissance may be carried out as far as the line Marieux-Puchevillers.'

These were the instructions which reached Richthofen on 20 April from the commander of his group. He knew that the matter was urgent, but not so urgent as to compel his personal intervention.

He did not intend to fly on 21 April, because he trusted No. 11 to deal with the 'strong opposition,' and he had so much business to do on the ground before he could leave with a clear conscience.

The sky was veiled in a thick haze which would prevent the German reconnaissance machines from fulfilling their mission, even if there were no Englishmen to stop them. It looked like a day of 'airmen's weather,' but Richthofen ordered his pilots to stand by in case it cleared. He sniffed the strong east wind that blew across the aerodrome, and it warned him that his machines would be heavily handicapped if they had to fight their way back.

But no English aircraft had been reported from the front, and the pilots of No. 11 were not worried about the east wind. Feeling in the best of spirits, they let off their superfluous energy in jovial horseplay.

Then the east wind suddenly blew the mist away, and Richthofen saw English machines over the front. If the weather was good enough for the enemy to fly, it was good enough for his pilots. He gave orders to take off.

Then he thought of the east wind again. The job was going to be more difficult than he originally anticipated, and he felt that he ought to see it through himself. 'Bring out my machine,' he commanded on a sudden impulse.

Then, just as he was buttoning up his overcoat, while one mechanic adjusted his helmet and another attended to his flying-boots, one of the eternal pressmen came up with his camera to snap the champion of eighty victories making ready for his eighty-first.

A shiver ran through the two mechanics and the bystanders. In the superstitions of the German airmen a photograph taken before a flight foreboded the very worst of all bad luck. Many an ignorant cameraman had been prevented just in time from committing this ill-omened act; if he succeeded in getting the photograph, nothing would induce its involuntary subject to take to the air on that occasion.

But Richthofen thought such fears childish, even though he had to recognise their effect on his subordinates. He determined to give them a lesson that day.

He turned his head and deliberately faced the cameraman.

Afterwards he saw a little dog playing at the entrance to a hangar. As he stooped to pat it, a sergeant came up with a postcard he had written to his son at home and asked him to sign it.

Richthofen smiled at him. 'Why are you in such a hurry?' he asked. 'Don't you think I'll come back?' Then he signed the postcard with the proffered fountain pen.

He led a group of five into the air. With him were Wolff and Karjus, two good men, and Sergeant-Major Scholz, who was not so experienced. The fifth pilot was another Richthofen – a cousin who had just joined the Staffel and was under strict injunctions to keep out of dogfights. They took off at about 11.30am.

Some time before their start, three Flights of No. 209 Squadron's Camels took off from Bertangles, about 20 miles away from Cappy. They occupied the same aerodrome from which Richthofen's most distinguished opponent had taken off to meet death at his hands.

After they had patrolled their area for a time without incident, a Flight of them dived away to attack a couple of two-seater Albatrosses, which were making for the lines. The other two Flights continued the patrol under the leadership of Captain A. Roy Brown, a Canadian.

Brown's primary purpose was to fight and destroy any German machines he might meet, but he also had a secondary one. He had made it his duty to look after his old school friend, Lieutenant W.R. May, who was a newcomer to the squadron. Like Richthofen's cousin, May had been ordered to keep out of dogfights.

Two of the machines led by Brown developed engine trouble and had to return, thus leaving him with only eight when he saw white shell-bursts away over to the west of Hammel.

The obvious inference he drew from them was that British anti-aircraft gunners were firing on German machines. He promptly led his two Flights in their direction; on reaching the scene of action, he found two RE8s from No. 3 FC (No. 3 Squadron, Australian Flying Corps), putting up a stout defence against some German machines which had attacked them when they were out on a photographic mission.

Richthofen had arranged for *Jagdstaffel* 11 to take off in two swarms, one of which he led himself, while Weiss took charge of the other. *Jagdstaffel* 5, which also went up that morning, met the third Flight of No. 209's Camels, and was hotly engaged with them over Sailly le Sec.

At first it seems an impossible task to sort out the details of the fight which took place when Brown's Camels came to the rescue of the two RE8s. As a German writer has aptly re-marked, the story of Richthofen's last moments in the air is now encrusted with as many legends as the mythical death of Siegfried. Some of the principal actors in the tragedy and a number of eye-witnesses have furnished accounts which appear contradictory on comparison, but this is only natural. The fleeting impressions on the brains of the pilots engaged in the fray are bound to be distorted, while many circumstances might affect the evidence of the men on the ground. Yet even the most difficult jig-saw puzzle must yield to patience and perseverance.

The following is, therefore, an attempt, submitted with all due diffidence, to solve a problem which cannot be insoluble.

When the fight began, Richthofen's swarm was outnumbered. Scholz had been unable to keep his place in the formation; he drifted over to join in the fighting in progress over Sailly le Sec, while Richthofen's cousin followed instructions and remained a spectator. But when Weiss's swarm and some Albatrosses joined in, the odds were against the Camels.

Then Brown found himself engaged in one of the hottest fights in which he had ever taken part. He did not expect to come out of it alive, but when he could spare a fleeting moment for a glance round, he saw that his machines were holding their own. Lieutenant J.W. Mackenzie set about a Fokker to such purpose that he forced it to retire before his own wounds made it necessary for him to leave, while Lieutenant F.J.W. Mellersh compelled another triplane to land at Cerisy. Mellersh was then attacked by Wolff, who put in an effective burst; he spun down for dear life and hedge-hopped home with his damaged machine.

Obedient to orders, May kept out of the dogfight, but when he saw a triplane hovering on the edge of the fray, he could not resist the temptation to attack it. But Richthofen's cousin was an even more obedient pupil and an even rawer novice than May. After firing a few shots in self-defence, he dived away, and made a bolt for Cappy.

May thrilled with delight ; he thought he had shot down his first Hun. Then he remembered instructions and put his machine into a turn in order to make for Bertangles.

Brown happened to catch a momentary glance of May's apparent success, and felt pleased about it for a tiny fraction of a second. Then he saw a red machine shoot out of the fight and start in pursuit of his friend.

Manfred von Richthofen was no more immune from erroneous impressions during a fight than any other pilot. Recognising by its markings the machine flown by the cousin who was under his special protection until he gained enough experience to look after himself, he made a dash at May. He meant to destroy him before he could follow his cousin down and finish him off.

Brown saw May's peril, but for the moment he could give him no help, because he was fighting three Fokkers for his life. He zig-zagged to spoil their aim, but when no way of escape seemed possible, he resolved to die fighting.

Collision! If he could force a collision with one or more of them he felt that at least he would gain the satisfaction of selling his life dearly. As two of them closed in on him, he went up in an Immelmann turn.

He saw them miss each other by inches; then he nearly got the third in his dive. As the other two came out of their turns, he zoomed up to their height again and let them attack him. At the last moment he passed out below them in a half-roll, and once again he saw the two opponents only just avoid the impact of collision!

Weiss had seen Richthofen pursuing May, but thought his commander could take care of himself, especially as Wolff was supposed to guard his tail. For the moment he was in charge of both swarms; all the German machines had lost height in the course of the fray, while the strong east wind had drifted them over the English lines. He gave the signal to return, imagining that Richthofen, who always combined prudence with audacity, would turn back in time if he failed to finish off his intended victim.

And so Brown found himself unmolested when he zoomed up for the third time. His first thought was for May.

He scanned the sky – no sign of him. He began to think his friend must have got home safely. Then, far away to northward, he saw a Fokker in pursuit of a Camel. And the Fokker was gaining on the fugitive!

Brown resumed his climb, in order to gain height for a long dive!

Wolff had started off in pursuit of Mellersh. Mindful of his self-imposed task of guarding Richthofen's tail, he looked round and saw the all-red machine following May. He was surprised to find it about to cross the lines at such a low height, for this was one of the dangers against which the commander had so often warned young airmen. He made up his mind to relinquish his pursuit of Mellersh and fly to Richthofen's aid. But before he could do so, he heard firing behind him. A Camel was on his tail, pumping lead into his machine.

He wriggled out of the enemy's fire, shook off his opponent and looked round again. But Richthofen had not returned; the only German machine in the vicinity was one which he recognised by its markings as belonging to Karjus. He flew over to him, but the persistent Camel came back and attacked them.

They chased it all the way to Corbie and then turned back. But there was still no sign of Richthofen; the all-red triplane had apparently vanished from the sky. Wolff began to feel worried.

May was zig-zagging to avoid his pursuer's bursts, but Richthofen hung on grimly. As usual, he held his fire until he was close enough for an accurate death-burst.

May thought he was lost. He ceased his zig-zags, risking everything in a straight, desperate dash for home. Richthofen also flew straight; he was too intent on his prey to look round, and so he never saw Brown climbing to gain height for the death-dive on to his tail.

At last he was only 30 yards behind May – nicely placed for a shot. His finger was on the trigger button, waiting to press it at the right moment.

The right moment came, but no bullets issued from his Spandaus. Both his guns refused to fire!

At once their failure brought him to a sense of his peril. He was now at a low height behind the enemy's lines and exposed to the fire of Corbie's anti-aircraft batteries, with a strong east wind to retard his progress home. A precarious enough position, even with serviceable weapons, to fight off any aerial opponent who tried to bar his way. But with jammed guns it was nothing less than hopeless.

As yet he had not seen the pursuing Camel behind him. His one thought was to get his machine out of range of those batteries. His right hand pulled at the stick; the all-red triplane began to climb.

Sergeant C.B. Popkin and Gunner R.F. Western, two Australians belonging to the 24th Machine Gun Company, were waiting behind their anti-aircraft gun in the corner of a wood, not far from Corbie. They saw the red triplane pursuing the Camel, but dared not fire until their own machine was clear of their sights. At last their gun spoke; from another position nearby, Gunner A. Franklyn also fired. An Australian staff officer, who happened to be in the wood at the time, heard the rattle of machine guns and saw the red triplane swerve. Elated at the prospect of a victim, other gunners took up the firing.

Richthofen's machine was hit. He switched off his engine and went into a glide. His holiday was gone; in its place a vista of long enforced idleness in captivity confronted him. But behind him was Brown's Camel.

When he had climbed a while, Brown glanced at his altimeter – 3,000 feet, height enough for a dive on to the red machine. He pushed his stick over and toed the rudder-bar for the sharp right-hand turn which was to bring him on to Richthofen's tail.

He did not see the red triplane climb and then go into a glide. If his eyes had taken in these movements, his brain would have failed to record them. His thoughts were all concentrated on the desperate necessity for overhauling the pursuer before he could put a burst into May's tail. It was therefore impossible for him to grasp the fact that the pilot in the triplane was a disarmed, disabled man with no alternative left but to land alive behind the English lines, if he could.

Brown fired. He saw his bullets rip Richthofen's elevator away and lacerate the Fokker's hinder parts. He pulled his stick and brought his machine up slightly; then he fired again.

This time he saw the red Fokker's pilot turn round and stare at him. He fancied he could see his eyes gleaming from behind his glasses. Then he saw him lurch forward in his seat, and, knowing that this enemy was now past all power to harm May, he ceased fire.

The all-red Fokker swerved to the right. Then it heeled over and plunged into the depths ...

Left in temporary charge of Cappy aerodrome, Reinhard waited for the return of the patrol. One by one the Fokker triplanes dropped down to rest, until at last all were safely accounted for except the pure red one.

At first Reinhard was not unduly alarmed. One pilot thought he had seen Richthofen's machine hard pressed by several opponents, but when he compared notes with the others, he was convinced that he had really seen Wolff in a tight corner. The general opinion was that Richthofen must have made a forced landing somewhere near the front lines, in which case he would be bound to ring up the aerodrome as soon as he reached the nearest telephone.

But half an hour passed without news of any kind. Then Leutnant Wenzl, a member of Weiss's swarm, remembered having seen a small machine on the ground behind the British lines and somewhere east of Corbie. He thought it looked to be painted red, but would not swear to its colour. Reinhard rang up the front and also sent up a chain of three machines to investigate.

'Where is Richthofen? Where is Richthofen?' was the message which passed up and down the line.

At last news came through. An artillery observer had seen a red triplane land on rising ground to the north of Vaux sur Somme. Khaki figures encircled it – he saw them carry a body from the machine, which they subsequently pulled to cover behind a rise in the ground. Later another message from the front said that Richthofen had been seen pursuing Camels, one of which he shot down. Then the remaining fugitive landed, and Richthofen's machine descended close to it . . .

Sergeant-Major J.H. Sheridan, of the third battery, RA, had also watched the fight. He had often seen other air-fights, but it was not so often that one had so close a view of the final act of a drama of the air. For a moment it looked as if the vanquished German was going to fall down right on top of him.

When it finally came to rest, he ran towards it, but the pilot made no effort to get out. His huddled body had pitched forward, so that his head rested on the end of a machine-gun, but his hand still clutched the stick. One glance was sufficient for Sheridan; he had seen that attitude before.

Men came running up, men of No. 3, AFC, then came a doctor. They lifted the body from the cockpit of the broken machine and laid it on the ground. They saw before them a handsome, clean-shaven young man, with lightish hair and a well-shaped head. There was blood on his face, and blood was clotting round a wound in his chest.

'Instantaneous death!' was the doctor's verdict.

Sheridan took the dead man's identity disc from his body and handed it to a pilot who had come down in the neighbourhood. Other hands searched the pockets, from which they took a gold watch engraved with the initials 'M v R' and a crest. There were also a number of papers.

They could not read the German sentences, but one of the documents looked to bear a resemblance to a pilot's certificate. They searched for the name, and then looked incredulously at the Fokker triplane for confirmation.

It was an all-red machine, relieved by no other colours save the black of the Maltese crosses which proclaimed its nationality, and the name on the document was Manfred von Richthofen! The greatest German ace had fallen at last!

It was the duty of Sergeant A.J. Porter, of No. 3, AFC to salve all aircraft which crashed or made forced landings in the neighbourhood of Bertangles. He had hastened from the aerodrome in his car as soon as the news came through that an enemy machine was down somewhere near Corbie. Under his directions five men helped him to raise the body, which they carried to the car. He also issued instructions for the machine to be removed to Bertangles, but the news of the pilot's identity ran round too quickly for him. Airmen, infantrymen, artillerymen hastened to take a look at it, and each of them wanted a souvenir for luck.

For luck! The luck of a machine which landed with a dead pilot inside would not be the best of luck, one might think, but the souvenir-hunters had a different point of view. They reasoned that the man who could last as long as Richthofen stood a good chance of seeing the war through! And so they stripped the wings, hacked at the woodwork and detached all removable metal parts, until there was little left for Porter's salvage party.

Meanwhile, Roy Brown had seen Mellersh chased by two Germans. Without landing to ascertain the fate of the machine he had shot down, he went to Mellersh's aid, and forced the Germans to abandon the pursuit. Then he returned to Bertangles, where he landed in a state of complete exhaustion after all his strenuous efforts. May was waiting to greet and thank him; they discussed the fight, but neither mentioned the name of Richthofen.

Both knew that the German champion flew an all-red machine, and the Fokker triplane which had pursued May and was pursued by Brown was red from nose to tail. The only possible inference was that Richthofen himself had flown it, but Brown dared not draw this inference. It seemed to him too great a presumption on his part.

He wrote out a terse combat report, stating that after extricating himself from the attacks of three German machines he had shot down a red triplane which was pursuing May. For this victory he cited his friend and Mellersh as witnesses.

But No. 209 Squadron had already heard the news. At lunch his messmates congratulated him on his victory over Germany's greatest airman, but he remained dubious. The feat seemed too incredible and impossible.

Just as they had finished the meal, Lieutenant-Colonel Cairns, the Wing-Commander, entered and asked Brown whether he really believed that he had shot Richthofen down. He did not seem at all pleased; Brown thought his manner cold and aloof.

He shook his head and repeated that he only claimed a red Fokker triplane. He had no idea who the pilot was.

Cairns looked uncomfortable and perplexed. The pilot was Richthofen; he could assure Brown that there was now no doubt on that point. But the trouble was that several Australian machine-gunners claimed to have shot him down, while an RE8 had also put in a claim. A bad business!

'Anyhow, I've got a car waiting,' he concluded. 'You'd better come along with me and see him!'

They drove to the headquarters of the 11th Australian Infantry Brigade, but neither felt inclined for conversation during the journey.

An Australian officer guided them to the spot where the body lay, guarded by several soldiers. It was just outside a hospital tent; when the news of Richthofen's death and the various claims had been telephoned through to the RAF headquarters, Brigadier-General Game gave instructions for all the evidence to be thoroughly sifted. The post-mortem examination conducted by several doctors had just been concluded.

Brown gazed on the frail, pathetic figure that lay before him. A kindly, wistful smile played about the delicate features.

An intense wave of depression overwhelmed the victor. He felt ashamed of himself; in his heart he cursed the war which had forced him to this unlucky deed. At that moment no price would have been too high for him to pay for the power to restore Richthofen to life.

Brown's agony was greater than he could bear. Unable to face the sight of his dead victim any longer, he strode to the car, where he waited in silence until Cairns was ready to drive him back to Bertangles.

The verdict of the doctors was unanimous Richthofen had been killed instantaneously by a bullet passing through his body at an angle which showed that it could not have been fired from the ground. The victory was awarded to Brown, and five days later an official statement was issued to that effect.

Porter took charge of the body on behalf of No. 209 Squadron and conveyed it to Bertangles in his car The funeral was fixed for the following afternoon, and the pilots of No. 209 were resolved to make it as worthy of the dead champion's career as the conditions of war permitted.

Meanwhile Richthofen lay in royal state. A large canvas hanger used by Porter was hastily cleared; in it they erected a dais, on which the body was laid. Pilots and mechanics from all the squadrons which used Bertangles aerodrome filed in to pay their respects to this most valiant enemy.

That night, Porter slept in the hanger with the body, which he prepared for the funeral. All through the following morning Bertangles aerodrome was the scene of many comings and goings. The ordinary work of the war still went on, but pilots from other squadrons, who could snatch the time from their duties, flew over with the flowers and wreaths which their squadrons had sent as tributes to the memory of the foeman they held in such high esteem. They, too, filed into the tent to look upon his face.

From his dais the dead Richthofen smiled at them all.

At 5 o'clock on this afternoon of 22 April a party of twelve men, headed by an officer, lined up before the entrance to the tent. Through the lane they formed, six squadron-leaders, all of whom had been decorated for their deeds in the aerial field of battle, entered and raised the coffin in which Richthofen's remains had been placed. They deposited it on a tender, where it was soon hidden from view by wreaths and flowers which surrounded it. One specially large wreath came from the headquarters of the Royal Air Force.

'To Captain von Richthofen, our valiant and worthy foeman,' was the inscription on it.

As the procession passed along the narrow country road, headed by an escort of Australian infantry, men in khaki paused from their normal occupations of war to salute the great foeman who could not escape the common lot. From camps beyond the meadows flanking the road, other men saw the cortège and stood to attention until it had passed out of sight.

From the corner of Bertangles cemetery where a grave had been dug under a hemlock tree, the eyes of the spectators could wander across a wide expanse of space to Amiens, where the mass of the cathedral stood out clear and beautiful in the mellow afternoon sun. On one side of this grave stood the pall-bearers with the coffin, on the other the firing-party, with the muzzles of their rifles grounded. Around them were many pilots who could claim to have exchanged shots with the dead airman, mechanics from Bertangles aerodrome in their stained overalls and a number of French civilians – women, children and old men past the age of military service. Beyond the hedge that bounded the cemetery stood rank upon rank of Australian infantry, while overhead aeroplanes circled round the grave.

Distant guns rumbled from the front as the army chaplain read the simple but impressive burial service. Then the pallbearers lowered the coffin into the earth; a sharp word of command broke the silence and twelve rifles were raised to fire the regulation three volleys which are the last tribute to a departed hero.

From Bertangles aerodrome Hawker had taken off to meet his death at Richthofen's hands. To Bertangles cemetery came Richthofen to sleep his last sleep. The wheel of Fate had rolled a full circle.

CHAPTER TEN

THE BATTLE OF 4 JUNE

By Compton Mackenzie

About 10 o'clock on the morning of 4 June, the destroyer *Wolverine* commanded by Lieutenant-Commander Adrian Keyes, the younger brother of the Commodore, took us from Kephalo to Helles. Besides Sir Ian Hamilton himself, there were General Braithwaite, Colonel Ward, Aspinall, Dawnay, and several others of the General Staff. We steamed for nearly an hour toward the sound of guns that was coming down through a grey and indeterminate kind of day which very gradually changed to a clearer atmosphere. A northerly wind was blowing, such a wind as might shatter the chestnut-blossom in England 'on some tempestuous morn of early June,' and most of us found the ward-room a pleasanter place than the deck. Keyes was full of stories about his experiences in Canada at the very beginning of the war, when he manned a submarine with a crew of local businessmen. I wish I could remember the details of the good stories he told us; but they have passed from my recollection irretrievably, and I can only remember the gold watch that was presented to him by his amateur crew. One of those Canadian businessmen ought to give us the tale of that sub-marine's adventures: *Blackwood's Magazine* would be the proper medium. Keyes himself is no longer alive, and the little epic ought not to be lost eternally. If I had not been so much worried at the time by the prospects of having to send the Press a despatch about the imminent battle, I might have remembered the stories myself.

When we drew near to Helles and went on deck, a fog of dust was blowing off the shore and the gun-crews were going to their stations, for the *Wolverine* intended to bring her guns to bear on the Turkish trenches. The men stripped to the waist for action sent my thoughts whirring back to the big engraving of the Death of Nelson which used to hang on our hall at home, and which in childhood I had studied many a time for an hour at a stretch, in fancy a powder-monkey of the Victory myself, on whose books I was now borne as a Marine. Then amongst the transports and trawlers and various craft at anchor we saw all that was now visible of the *Majestic* like a small green whale motionless upon the water. She was subsiding rapidly, they said; and already in this watery sunlight she gave the illusion of slowly assuming to herself the nature of the waves that splashed against her still rigid sides. Such a dream of a ship's transmutation into her own element soon vanished in the billows of dust ashore, vanished in that queer heartlessness of war that is really the desperate occupation of the mind with something to do and therefore no time to dream. And yet there were still left a few moments to dream while we waited for the lighter to come alongside, and I was saying to myself that Lancashire Landing, the glorious name the Lancashire Fusiliers won for W beach, was the climax of all the castles in the sand that were ever built. No children at Blackpool or at Southport could ever have imagined in their most ambitious schemes this effect of grown-up industry. The comparison with a seaside resort on a fine bank holiday arrived so inevitably as really to seem rather trite. Yet all the time the comparison was justifying itself. Even the aeroplanes on the top of the low cliff eastward had the look of an 'amusement' to provide a threepenny or sixpenny thrill: the tents might so easily conceal phrenologists or fortune-tellers: the signal station might well be a *camera obscura*: the very carts of the Indian Transport, seen through the driven sand, had an air of waiting goat-carriages.

General Gourad was on the sandbagged pier expecting Sir Ian Hamilton, as grave as one of those bearded French *maîtres d'hôtel* who has prepared a marvellous banquet for an important personage. We walked up the slope from the beach, blinded by the dust, choking, thinking of nothing except this dust, until there broke upon me the realisation that all this time the guns had been thundering. Suddenly an empty stretch of desiccated scrub rolled away before us: the homely clatter of the beach was forgotten: there was nothing now but a noise of wind rising above the battery we were leaving behind us: and for the eye nothing but the black and white telegraph poles, their wires winking in the sun, and the imperturbable larks rising and falling. This empty stretch began on the skyline, and it was soon necessary to enter a trench originally dug by the Turks, good enough, it seemed, to withstand any but the heroes of that imperishable assault upon 25 April. We hurried on, here and there almost sticking in the rank clay that was sometimes even wet enough to require a mattress of boughs for its passage. Finally we reached the 'shelter' which was considerably labelled 'Low Doorway' upon the lintel: there always seems something a little pathetic in these minor courtesies of war. The shelter consisted of four or five compartments hollowed out of the clay, and covered with sandbags over a ceiling of corrugated iron. The walls were hung with canvas, and each of the low oblong windows, as we leaned upon their high sills, provided a new aspect, framed in branches, of the battle 3 miles away. Somewhere behind us a 60-pounder crashed at intervals: and we could hear the moan and rattle of the shell go forward on its way.

In front of the shelter, the country dipped gradually down to rise again more steeply beyond a wide and partially wooded hollow. Here, through the glasses, could be seen a quantity of mules tranquil enough, notwithstanding the concentration of shell-fire that was sweeping and shrieking and buzzing over their heads to explode half-way up the opposite slope. Every shell burst with its own shape of smoke; and so substantial was the vapour that the wind could only carry it away bodily, unable for a long time to disperse it. The shrapnel puffs materialised from the air at first as small and white wads of cotton-wool; then they grew swiftly larger and turned to a vivid grey; then they became fainter again and travelled across the view like tadpoles of cloud, until at last they trailed their tails in a kind of fatigue before they dissolved against the sky. Heavy shells evoked volcanoes right along the line, and from the sea, like drums solemnly beaten, came the sound of the ships firing.

The calm within the shelter was oppressive, though the wind was fretting the grass and fluttering two magenta cistus flowers immediately outside the window. It seemed calm as we looked at the maps pegged out upon the trestle-tables; but it was 11.50, and at 12.00 the advance would begin. A tortoise crawled laboriously past our straining binoculars. The gun-fire lessened, and from the whole line the noise of musketry and maxims came sharply, a noise that was tenser than the guns, and more portentous. It was as though one had been listening to a change of orchestration in a symphony, as though after a heavy and almost dull opening the strings were leading to a breathless finale of the first movement.

Yet, at 12 o'clock, as we stared through our glasses, there was scarcely any sign of action. Once indeed a large body of men were visible as they climbed the green slope; but they were soon lost to view, and notwithstanding the incessant scolding of the angry rifle-fire, we had nothing at which we could look except the mules standing motionless in the hollow, and once down a ribbon of road an orderly galloping. Yet all the time messages were coming in along the wires; all the time it was possible to mark with green and red and blue pencils a redoubt gained, a trench occupied, or at some point a check.

One of those fatal checks was to the 6th Gurkhas who had found the barbed wire to the left of the Saghir Deré untouched by the bombardment. The Saghir Deré was a ravine west of Krithia which began in the sandy cliffs to the south-west of the Peninsula, where the Headquarters of the 29th Division were now established. The sides were covered with a thick tangle of brushwood and ran down, sometimes sheer from a height of 50 feet, into a narrow bottom full of arbutus and the stones of a dried-up watercourse.

On the morning of the battle the 88th Brigade held the country to the right; on the left was the Indian Brigade which included the Lancashire Fusiliers. The 14th Sikhs were astride the ravine linking their own Brigade, the 6th Gurkhas on the left, with the Worcesters, who formed the left of the 88th Brigade, by a line of trenches about 150 yards wide.

On the west above the ravine the ground, matted with heather, cistuses, and various stunted shrubs, sloped upwards toward two lines of Turkish trenches which confronted us from a distance of 200 yards and 350 yards. On the east beyond our trenches the ground sloped downwards to the edge of the ravine from a crest line about 200 yards away, the distance between the two lines of trenches being 250 yards. Both the Turks and our men had been using the ravine itself as a communicating trench with the rear. This piece of ground was unfortunately exposed by its aspect to the fire not only of the trenches in front, but more dangerously to that of the powerful trenches on the other side of the Saghir Deré, which dominated not only the ravine itself, but also the open ground eastward up to the crest line.

This morning the Sikhs had been ordered to advance in two lines. The front line was to link the attack of the Indian Brigade with that of the 88th Brigade by moving forward along the sides of the ravine, and so by a flank attack help the assault upon the trenches opposed to the Indian Brigade. The second line was to advance along the ravine to attack the second line of the enemy's trenches. The Turks had placed several small trenches across the bottom of the ravine, and there were probably several machine guns well-hidden on the steep slopes.

After that bombardment, which ran from sea to sea, the Allied line advanced at noon. On the right of the Saghir Deré the 88th Brigade went forward with complete success, and the Worcesters, who were in touch with the Sikhs, actually charged through four lines of Turkish trenches as easily as Aspinall and Dawnay were marking down with coloured pencils their achievement on the map. The Sikhs, however, came full into the cross-fire of rifles and machine guns as they moved over the exposed slope. Nevertheless the two companies did not falter in their determination, but kept pace with the advance of the Brigade. Notwithstanding their losses on the slope downward to the edge of the Saghir Deré they reached the Turkish trenches, carried them, and bayoneted the occupants, who tried to escape into the ravine. All day and night these two companies held the left of the trenches taken by the 88th Brigade, and in the morning when they were relieved there remained one British officer, one Indian officer, and fourteen men.

Down in the ravine the day went badly for the Sikhs. The 6th Gurkhas on their left had failed to carry the first line of Turkish trenches and their web of barbed wire which the guns from the ships had left untouched. Relieved from anxiety from the Gurkhas the enemy was free to concentrate a violent fire on the attack up the Saghir Deré. Machine guns opened on them from both sides at the moment they came out of their trenches. Four British officers and a quarter of the rank and file fell at once. A few groups gloriously led managed to clamber to the point at which they hoped to see the two companies of their first line in hot assault upon the enemy's trenches. But when with tremendous effort they arrived they saw that the frontal attack on their left had failed. Some dead ground gave them time to muster the survivors: a scar in the ravine was stormed: two machine guns were dragged up: entrenchments were desperately dug: and thus they perched upon the side of the Saghir Deré – the Colonel, the Doctor, and forty-seven men. There all through the night they held on; but in the morning the Turks from above bombed them back into the ravine. The crews of the guns had been killed, and, though the guns had to be abandoned, all that was left of the second line retired in good order. A bomb destroyed one gun: the other was afterwards recovered.

The other two companies of the first line had advanced with the rest of their own Brigade against the trenches in front of them; but when the main attack had failed, they would not go back. All day by the edge of the Saghir Deré did they cling to their position; and when at last they retired, they left three-quarters of their strength and every British officer behind.

That morning the 14th (King George's Own) Sikhs moved out to the attack with fifteen British officers, fourteen Indian officers and

514 men. On the morning after, three British officers, three Indian officers, and 134 men were left. No ground was given: no man turned his back: no man lingered on the way. The trenches of the enemy that ran down into the ravine were choked with the bodies of Turks and Sikhs, lying there for ever at rest from that hell of hand-to-hand encounters. On the slope beyond, the bodies of those tall and grave warriors, all face downward where they fell indomitably advancing, lay thickly among the stunted aromatic scrub. Achi Baba was before them, and eastward the sun was rising out of Asia.

Standing there in the shelter, I saw Aspinall's face gnawed by anxiety as he pored over that check on the pegged-out map, knowing no more then of the history of it which I have just related than I did myself. Probably I felt awkwardly superfluous in the presence of his anxiety, for I know that soon after this I found myself in another compartment of the shelter with a naval officer beside me, who explained a little apologetically that he had come ashore as ADC to the Commodore and had been given leave to look at the battle from the shelter. We chatted for a while, and presently he asked me if I had come out here from Flanders. I was gratified by the implication that I looked such a veteran, but admitted that I had as a matter of fact only come out here from Italy a few weeks ago.

'Oh, really? I'm frightfully keen on Italy,' he avowed with enthusiasm. 'I wonder if you know Capri by any chance?'

'That's where I live.'

'I wonder if you know an uncle of mine, Colonel Palmes? I stayed with him in Capri two years ago. And now I want to get back there again to meet a man called Mackenzie. Do you know him?'

'Well, I think I must be the Mackenzie you mean.'

'The man who wrote *Sinister Street*? Well, that's absolutely extraordinary! Do you know, I've had the two volumes of *Sinister Street* with me ever since February. I've read them both through at least three times, and some parts a good deal more than three times. I saved them from going down in a torpedo-boat which was sunk under me, and I've saved them from going down in a trawler which was sunk under me. The TB was on the Canal.'

I remembered the tale of the exploits of TB 043 on the Suez Canal, for the uncle of its gallant commander (Commander G.B. Palmes, DSO, RN) had told me about that nephew of his who had just been given the DSO. We stood in that shelter and gazed at one another with frank admiration while the sixty-pounder crashed and moaned away behind

and the magenta cistus flowers fluttered by the sill in the wind outside.
I asked him what he was doing in these waters.

'Oh, I'm in charge of the mine-sweepers out here. But I thought that
was a good chance to get ashore for a day. So I asked the Commodore
to trot me along as his ADC.'

Just then Colonel Ward looked in to say that fifty prisoners were
coming in on our left, and asked me if I would like to walk along with
him to meet them. I never saw Palmes again while I was at Gallipoli,
and I have never met him since on Capri or anywhere else; but the
memory of that ten minutes' talk fourteen years ago is still perfectly
fresh.

The greyness of the morning had vanished by now, and the air
outside was brilliant after the damp and gloom of the shelter when
Colonel Ward and I started off along the road which ran by the cliff's
edge towards the line of battle. Out at sea, escorted by destroyers,
Albion and *Implacable*, their guns spurting vivid yellow from turrets
that stood in blackest silhouette against the dazzle of the sea and the
silver fume of the horizon, were streaming up and down at their slow
and stately business and their solemn firing.

We met the escort of Worcesters just where a Red Cross flag was
flying above the cliff burrows of the Field Ambulance. Some of the
prisoners were badly wounded; these were at once taken off for
medical attention. The rest were halted, and several of the Worcesters
came literally dancing round us, not yet free from that first wild elation
of their charge. The dust and sweat caked upon their faces made it
almost impossible to see where the khaki ended and the flesh began:
they seemed like the clay models of a sculptor: and their bayonets
lacked even so much lustre as tarnished foil. They were like children
drunk with the thrills of some unusual adventure, as they skipped
round us in their shorts, laughing and chattering of the deeds of their
regiment; and the plaster of dust obliterating all lines, all hair, all signs
of age, made them appear more than ever like children. In contrast to
their jubilation I see a tall ungainly Turk in his ill-fitting khaki uniform
who looks at me in despair. I realise that he wants to step out of the
ranks to make water. I nod assent, and, whether he has hurt himself
internally or whether too long retention is the cause, the business is an
agony, for he stands twisted in a fearful cramp, his face showing what
he is suffering not by any contortions, but by such dumb pain as you
may see in the eyes of an animal. I turn away sick at heart for him, and

then one of the merry Worcesters dances round me and babbles once more his excited tale of a few minutes' madness.

'My gawd, sir, we went through them like paper. Four trenches, sir. Like paper. With the bayonet. Right through, sir! At the double. Like paper. Four trenches, sir, you wouldn't believe! At twelve to the tick. Like paper. Four trenches! Well, I can't say I hardly knew what I was doing, or where I was going, and that's a fact. And then we found we'd took four trenches! That's right, ain't it, Nobby? Four trenches, sir. Coo! It was a treat the way we got into 'em. You know, sir? It was as good as a football match. Four trenches! Well, nothing couldn't stop us.'

'I say, Mackenzie,' broke in the slow voice of Colonel Ward. 'Do you think you can make out what regiment these fellows belong to?' I produced the War Office's handbook for fighting against Turkey, and after examining the numerals I felt fairly sure that it was a '15' on their collars. I decided to risk it, and going up to the prisoners who were all squatting down by the roadside now, I inquired: *'Umbesh alai?'*

Ali Baba could not have felt more astonished when he said: 'Open Sesame' and the door of the Forty Thieves' cave actually did open, for I had no sooner spoken than all the prisoners leapt to their feet and saluted. They were beaming with excitement, and evidently most anxious to go on with the conversation. But to say '15th Regiment' in Turkish was as much as I could manage, and the conversation had to stop there, leaving the prisoners and myself smiling at one another, until Deedes, his puragee fluttering behind him, came hurrying up to examine them. The Turks were evidently delighted to have been taken, and they answered Deedes's questions with enthusiasm, while squatting there in the dusty scrub, many of them wounded, but none complaining, and all of them grinning and nodding at the cigarettes their escort kept handing to them. It was impossible to examine the prisoners here more than cursorily, because a group so large might have drawn the enemy's fire: so they were presently marched down toward Lancashire Landing and the accommodation of the Assistant-Provost-Marshal, their delightful captors dancing along beside them like children bringing home some stray cows to the farm where they belonged.

When we went back in the shelter, there was still nothing visible of the battle's progress, and it was Aspinall, I think, whom I accompanied down to the Headquarters of the Twenty-ninth Division. Here heralded by the telephone's petulant and gnat-like buzz, more details of the battle were coming in. The Worcesters were holding fast to those trenches they had captured. Thinking of the men in that escort who had danced about in the road by the cliff's edge and chattered all together like children about their exploits, I took a ridiculous personal pride in the red lines that marked their achievement. Here I first heard definite news of the losses that the Indian Brigade had suffered by the Saghir Deré, though the full story of their desperate fight was of course still to be told. I heard, too, for the first time how the French had failed to hold the Haricot Redoubt on the right of the Naval Division, which had suffered a bloody enfilade in consequence from the three tiers of trenches banked one above the other on the slope of the Kereves Deré. And it was here I first heard a whisper that the Collingwood Battalion had been obliterated as a ship is sunk with all hands. At 4 o'clock General Gourard sent word that an attempt would be made to retake the Haricot. My companion looked graver and graver. Unless the French succeeded it would be necessary to order back the Manchester Brigade, which was half-way up to the top of Achi Baba, but alas, with its right flank exposed, for the Naval Division had been unable to advance and establish contact with these Lancashire Territorials owing to the failure of the French which had left another right flank exposed. Sir Ian Hamilton had been sneered at for claiming that we were within an ace of victory. Yet if a small entanglement of barbed wire on the left of our line had not escaped the ships' guns and if troops more reliable than the Senegalese had been on the right of it, Achi Baba would have fallen a few days later and the casualties of the Fourth of June would not have been a quarter of what they were.

Yes, it was Aspinall whom I had accompanied to Divisional Head-quarters, for as I strain to recapture that afternoon fourteen years later the very expression on his face comes back to me as we emerged from the dug-outs to walk gloomily back along the paths winding among the tents and cavities, paths that the Irishmen of the Dublins and Munsters had found time to decorate with carefully chosen white stones. Once more returned that sensation of being near the seaside and of all this noise of battle being but a dream.

The rifles and maxims had begun again when we reached the shelter. That second advance timed to begin at 4 o'clock was already in full swing. Again we tried to see the figures of men in their bayonet charges up the slope: and still there was nothing visible except the mules, and an ambulance waggon galloping up that ribbon of road.

The sun was by now westering fast, and the shelter was lit up with a nimbus of pale gold.

The second advance had not achieved what was hoped for. The Manchester Brigade must be ordered to retire. A black depression fell. I stood aside for Sir Ian Hamilton to pass back along the trench. Then with one glance over my shoulder at that accursed hill of Achi Baba which still stood with hunched defiant shoulders between us and Constantinople, I followed the single file procession down the trench. Nobody spoke a word. Birds were twittering in their flight through the radiant air, and beyond them three biplanes went winging home-ward to Tenedos, one behind the other, as birds fly across the sunset to roost. The sixty-pounder was still moaning on its way to the enemy's lines; but neither gunshot nor gloomy thoughts could quite destroy the amber peace of that evening of the Fourth of June.

It was when we were waiting near the pier that Guy Dawnay and I saw those wounded men of the Naval Division coming down tired and silent to the beach to embark in a lighter and go on board a hospital ship. And when, as I have already related, he told me to move along out of their way, because they would not want to be seeing us, I knew how bitterly he was thinking of those green and red and blue lines on the maps pegged down to those trestle-tables in the shelter up there behind us. I think that we talked about Eton on the voyage back, and I seem to remember that Aspinall joined us in some quiet corner and that he and Dawnay looked at one another without speaking. Anyway, I know that when we stepped ashore on the soft beach of Kephalo I felt that a long century lay between the flushed twilight in which we came back and the grey morning when we started.

On Monday, the seventh of June, there was a chance of crossing again to Helles in a destroyer. I welcomed an excuse to escape from the stifling atmosphere of the tent which had been full of blood-stained Turkish notebooks for the last two days, and asked leave to visit my Divisional Paymaster to discuss the problem of my pay and at the same time try for a batman. The atmosphere at Divisional Head-quarters was gloomy in the extreme. I was not astonished when I heard details of what the Division had been through last Friday. The casualties had been very heavy. They thought that the French had let them down completely on the right. Patrick Shaw-Stewart was seen running along, waving his cane and shouting: 'Avancez! Avancez!' The Senegalese came out of their trenches, advanced 17 yards, and then bolted back into them like so many gigantic black rabbits, after which nothing would persuade them to show themselves again. I suppose this was after the Colonial troops and Senegalese had been bombed out of the Haricot Redoubt which they had held for a time. There was no disposition to put any blame for the failure of the Fourth of June on the General Staff. Any gibing was mostly directed at Maxwells' *Peninsula Press* which had come out with a rosified account of our 'success', though of course it was recognised that a daily sheet of unmitigated gloom would hardly be worth printing and circulating. I was promised a batman; but the problem of my pay looked like being for ever insoluble, and I started to walk back. Small shells kept dropping all round me, and it seemed inevitable that I should be hit presently. There is no doubt that the sensation of being shelled when alone is most infernally unpleasant. After walking about three-quarters of a mile I felt inclined to sit down and cry with exasperation because those Turkish gunners would not realise that I really was not worth so much expensive ammunition. I wanted to argue with them personally about the futility of war. It seemed so maddeningly stupid that men should behave as impersonally and unreasonably as nature. Over to the right I saw a clump of trees and, feeling I simply must somehow get a sensation of cover, I hurried across toward them at a diagonal jog-trot. I could not have made a more foolish move, because apparently there was a well by them at which mules were watered, and at regular intervals the enemy used to spray the clump with shrapnel. I must have come in for one of those antiseptic douches, for the air was alive. I began to worry about the proofs of *Guy and Pauline*, thinking to myself that the printer's reader would be sure to change 'tralucent' to 'translucent' and that Secker in the depression caused by the news of my death would never remember how much importance I attached to getting rid of that unnecessary sibilant. Why couldn't those blasted Turks up on Achi Baba shut up? And I would have turned a gerund into a participle here and there ... and probably there would be a vile *nominativus pendens* ... (a noun phrase, introduced as if the subject of a sentence, that is not actually used as such) at this moment I heard a burst of laughter and, looking angrily, for I thought this laughter must be meant for the way I was definitely running by now, I saw a couple of men digging opposite to one another like the gravediggers in Hamlet and roaring with laughter every time one of the small shells either exploded or as often happened hit the ground with a thud and nothing else. Then one of the pair dropped. The other looked first at his pal and then at me who was hurrying past with haversack, water-bottle, pistol, and glasses jogging up and down in a most undignified way.

'Beg pardon, sir! Beg pardon!' he called out.

'You can't do anything,' I snapped. 'You'd better get into cover yourself as quickly as you can.'

'No, sir, it's not that,' he whimpered as he cut across my path and forced me to stop while he saluted. 'But would you mind telling me if my friend's dead, sir, because I'm new at this job.'

'Of course, I'm not bloody well dead, you silly little cod,' shouted the friend, who was sitting up by now and rubbing his head. And I left them, remembering another occasion when the friend actually had been killed and when the survivor's comment was: 'Beg pardon, sir, you think it's funny at first, but it's very serious really.'

By the time I reached the beach, the big gun on the Asiatic side of the Straits had started to shell the shipping. There were three preliminary fountains, after which a shell hit a French transport loaded with hay. The crew at once jumped overboard, and the transport caught fire. Then two destroyers rushed up and bundled all the men back on to their ship in order to extinguish the fire, which they succeeded in doing without being shelled any more.

I think it must have been that evening I met the last surviving officer of the Collingwood Battalion. He was very young, hardly more than eighteen and, after the horror of that experience to which he had gone almost within forty-eight hours of landing at Helles, he was being sent to do some work at Imbros in connection with the rest camp which was to be formed there. We did not talk about the battle, either then or at any other time. Oldfield was his name, and I hope he survived the battles in France later. I can hear now the tone of his voice as he said to me with a nervous little laugh: 'I'm the only officer left of the Collingwood.'

CHAPTER ELEVEN

THE SECOND BATTLE OF YPRES

By Lieutenant-Colonel L.A. Strange, DSO, MC, DFC

Although I flew Martynside and Bristol Scout machines on many occasions, the specialisation of airmen into fighters, bombers, scouts, etc., had not yet taken place, for the simple reason that aerial warfare was still in its early stages. An airman was, therefore, in that April of 1915 more or less the same 'maid of all work', that he had been in August 1914 and I had to do my share of long reconnaissances in a BE2c. Lieutenants Hawkins, Morton, and De Halpert, and Captain Bovill, were some of my observers at that time, and we were usually about two and half hours in the air, reconnoitring the area around Langemarck, Dixmude, Roulers, Thielt, Courtrai, Menin, and Lille.

I remember one very uncomfortable trip with De Halpert. It started badly, because an anti-aircraft gunner got in a good shot, and a piece of HE, which caught me in the neck, made a painful scratch. It started just like a sting from an extra vicious wasp, but I grinned and bore it until we were at the far end of our area, when we were attacked by two German aircraft which carried machine guns. One of them looked most formidable; I forget its name, but it was a twin engine with a double fuselage. In the middle of the fight, one cylinder of the Renault engine carried by our BE2c cut out altogether, and as we were flying at only 4,000 feet, I knew it would need very careful handling if we were to get back across the 50-odd miles of airway that separated us from our lines. I imagine that we ought to have been fairly easy victims for those Germans, but when they saw us turn back they evidently thought their honour satisfied by forcing us to retreat, and so they let us have a shot for home unmolested.

We struggled painfully back, until we reached Menin, where we were literally smothered in shellfire from the Archies there. The black and white bursts around us looked a solid mass, and the din was terrific, but we could do nothing but plod steadily onwards as we were now down to 2,000 feet and still losing height. Holes began to appear in the fabric of our wings, while the oil-pressure gauge went down to nil and the engine started vibrating badly. Then I suddenly saw a tear appear on the shoulder of De Halpert's flying jacket and thought he must have been wounded.

Our next bit of trouble occurred when a lump of shrapnel smashed the rev. counter in my cockpit, but I suppose I ought to have looked on it as a blessing in disguise, because it mercifully put me out of the agony of watching the engine revs. gradually drop back. But all bad times come to some sort of end at last, and so we scraped over the trenches at about 500 feet, and were thankful to land behind a small wood just out of range of any serious shelling. To my relief I found that De Halpert was unwounded, a splinter of shell having torn his coat without grazing his skin; but we were both annoyed to have had such a rotten trip to no purpose, as it was too misty on the ground for us to see enough to make out any sort of report.

I also took part in sundry bombing operations. We now had a supply of French bombs, twenty-five pounders, which seemed nice little presents for the enemy, and one day I managed to drop three of these on Courtrai railway station. I dropped down to 100 feet to be sure of my target and managed to hit a train. I could not be sure of the extent of the damage, but later reports came in from secret agents to state that I had hit a troop train, while the subsequent mess I had made of the station had held up all traffic for the next three days.

On 22 April I was cruising up and down over the Salient with Lieutenant Hawkins. We were watching out for gun flashes in the fading light when suddenly my attention was attracted by what appeared to be streams of yellowish-green smoke coming from the German front line trenches.

This was such a strange phenomenon that we promptly dropped down to 2,000 feet to have a good look at it. At first I was completely puzzled, but finally my brain connected it with the rumours we had heard about the German preparations for using poison gas. About ten days previously a German soldier, captured by the French prior to the attack on Hill 60, had told his captors about a big attack planned for the Ypres area, when a deadly gas was to be used. The information duly reached British headquarters, and one day our No. 6 Squadron had received orders to search for signs of preparation for this attack. We had discovered nothing, and were inclined to look upon the rumour as something that had originated in the aforesaid prisoner's brain.

But now we thought otherwise, and, as a matter of fact, we had seen the beginning of the first German gas attack which nearly gave the game into the enemy's hands. We did not bother about our job any more, but raced back full throttle to Poperinghe, where we were bustled into a tender and taken straight to the Fifth Corps Headquarters to report personally to General Plumer. He questioned us very closely about what we had seen, and we realised that things were going to be serious.

Quite how serious I do not think we appreciated. The next morning I was up in the air before daybreak, taking Captain Harold Wyllie over the Salient in order to ascertain what had happened during the night, as soon as there was sufficient light to see by. To our amazement we could find no signs of troops in the usual trenches, but soon discovered a new front line of trenches about 4 or 5 miles nearer Ypres. Whether these were occupied by French or Germans it was impossible to tell from the heights, but as soon as we dropped down low enough we obtained ample evidence that this new line, extending from Boesinghe to St Julien, was held by the enemy. Wyllie hastily sketched it in his map and then we hurried back; by 8.30am we were at GHQ, where we expressed our apprehension of the fact that we had failed to discover any traces of British troops confronting the Germans in their new positions. We wondered why the latter had taken the trouble to dig themselves in, when, as far as we could see, there was nothing to prevent them continuing their advance.

All our machines spent many hours in the air that day, bombing the new trenches and the German reserves concentrated about Langemarck and Zarren. Hawker was especially active, but at the end of a long day's work he was wounded in the foot by rifle fire from the ground.

Our busy day was followed by a disturbed night, as French Colonial troops were retreating in masses along the road that led past our aerodrome. The first warning we had of their presence came from the rifle of our sentry at the end of the road, a newly-joined mechanic who dutifully called out: 'Halt! who goes there?' to the advancing rabble. As the reply he obtained was unsatisfactory – probably owing to his ignorance of any language but his own – and as he knew that the enemy's attack had been successful, and thought he might expect the Huns any moment, he decided to take no chances and blazed away to the best of his ability. The guard turned out, and as they were equally suspicious of the intruders, a lively engagement with our coloured allies seemed imminent. But suddenly loud whistling shrieks sang over our heads, while four crashes on the aerodrome announced the fact that we were under shell-fire; being unaccustomed to such attentions from the enemy's artillery, we forgot our argument with the darkies and sought shelter in the best available cover.

The French Colonials carried on with their retirement. From what we saw of them, they appeared to be a motley, disorderly crew, and they were evidently far too scared to put up much of a protest against our objections to their presence. In fact, their retreat was something more akin to a rout, but in their excuse it must be urged that if this gas warfare was uncanny to us, it was doubly so to them. It was not at all the sort of fighting they had come all the way from Africa to take part in.

We were shelled off and on all the night, consequently the enthusiasm of our pilots and observers for reconnaissances and artillery observation in the early hours of the morning was more apparent than usual. We wanted to get our own back on the long range gun that had disturbed our night's rest, but it was so cleverly concealed at Pilkem that it took us several days of very close searching before we found it. Meanwhile, however, this gun got on to our hangars about 11.30 that morning and held up work for nearly half an hour, after which the authorities decided to move us back to Abeele.

Poperinghe was a most interesting town in the early part of 1915, but I fancy its brightest spot was a certain inn (my truant memory has forgotten the name) where one could see the remnants of the old British Army mixing with the first drafts of Kitchener's recruits and listen to their conversation.

The 'Old Contemptibles' were generally rather grim and somewhat unresponsive to the eager questions and warlike enthusiasm of the men fresh from England. When the latter inquired: 'What's it like up there; tell us all about it!' the reply they generally got was a curt: 'Oh, you'll soon find out all about it. Don't worry yourself till you get there.'

But when pipes and cigarettes were lit after a good meal, you had a chance to listen to some curious conversations. At a table in a corner, perhaps, a couple of gunners might be discussing the situation with some members of a crack cavalry regiment. As neither lot had seen their beloved horses for weeks, mud, trench feet, snipers, the latest type of trench mortar, parapet repairs, and barbed wire formed the usual topics, each of which drew forth forcible expressions of fervent disgust from the talkers. They seemed to take such incidents of trench warfare as a studied insult to cavalry; while the gunners complained of the monotony of having to fire the same silly old number of rounds per day from the same adjectival old spot at the same blankety blank old map square, meanwhile expressing grave doubts of the efficiency of gunfire directed by some funny bloke perched high up above them in a funny aeroplane, who probably knew nothing whatever about guns. In indignant tones they asked what other surprises this disgusting war had in store for self-respecting Royal Horse Artillerymen.

Then the conversation would drift back to those far-off days of the retreat from Mons. Yes, that was some sort of a war, everyone would agree, whereupon somebody would recall an incident at La Fére, when two squadrons of Uhlans were wiped out. That would bring forth a story about the way in which a certain Sergeant-Major Grant had decapitated a heavy German trooper who was shouting: 'Kamerad, kamerad! I vas a vaiter at ze Ritz,' as both rode hell for leather over a fence into a cottage garden. The unfortunate German's head fell into a chicken run, causing much agitation among the poultry; but Grant with commendable promptness rescued a couple of good chickens from bad company and enjoyed their better acquaintance when he had some leisure. Whether the chickens enjoyed it is extremely doubtful.

Then someone would be moved to relate the story of No. 1's gun crew in 'L' Battery at Compiegne, when they fired at point blank range and cut ghastly lanes through masses of grey-green infantry for two solid hours and more. Just when they could fire no more they were galloped back to safety by an odd team brought up by that self-same Sergeant-Major Grant, who had noticed their plight when making a desperate effort to get a message through to a battalion that was ordered to retire from an isolated position. But these and other epic stories of those stirring times should be placed on record by those who witnessed the events. Most of them, alas, are jealously guarded in regimental and battery chronicles.

But to return to my own share in the war, we spent a record number of hours in the air on the day that Poperinghe aerodrome was shelled. According to my diary it was a most anxious time, while my personal efforts comprised five and a half hours' flying. From the air we could see heavy fighting round Langemarck, where the Canadians put up a stout resistance in a desperate position. For several days the situation was critical, but I imagine that the German failure to break through was due to the fact that the enemy was too surprised by the first success to follow it up properly, and so we gained time to adopt counter measures.

In the early months of 1915, the RFC played its part to the best of its ability; but it must be remembered that flying was in its infancy, while the trenches running from the sea to the Swiss frontier were a novelty in warfare. Looking back on these days, one realises that a great deal more might have been done to assist the hard-pressed troops in the Salient, if only we had had a little more experience of this type of fighting. But after all, we had our difficulties to master, as well as many special jobs, such as dropping baskets of carrier pigeons to secret agents at selected spots, and landing the agents themselves behind the enemy lines, which was a very ticklish business. No. 6 lost Captain Mulcahy-Morgan, who was taken prisoner on one of these jobs.

Although we had to carry out long-distance reconnaissances every day, and had a lot of photography and wireless work, flights in the air gradually became more frequent. My diary records the fact that we drove down six enemy aircraft between 26 April and 8 May.

But it was still difficult to engage the Germans in the air, as their pilots declined combat whenever they could. In his masterly work, *Deutschlands Krieg in der Luft* (Germany's War in the Air), General Hoeppner complains of the inferiority of German machines, both as regards arms and flying speed, and says that their losses were so great that the pilots received orders to retreat when an Entente machine came into sight. The Germans had, however, one great advantage over us, as the height at which their machines flew was gradually increased. In the spring of 1915 they seldom crossed the lines at anything lower than 8,000 feet, which was 2,000 or 3,000 feet above our usual height.

Whenever I encountered a Hun whilst flying my Martynside, I always had a frightful struggle to force myself up to 8,000 feet. Meanwhile the enemy would be steadily climbing, and although I found that our respective positions in the air generally suited the Martynside's angle of fire, I never got a chance of a surprise attack on an unsuspecting foeman.

The German machines gained their height behind their own lines, and then came across somewhere near the top of their 'ceiling', which was about as high as our own, or maybe a bit higher. Consequently they had plenty of chances to spot any attacks we planned on them, with the result that they were usually well behind their own lines again before we could get near them. Then they just dived for their aerodromes; we dived too, as soon as we saw them begin to go down, so as to try and cut them off when they had to cross our level, but generally their extra height gave them an extra speed that took them safely down.

But on 10 May 1915, I reached 8,500 feet when going after an Aviatik belonging to von Leutser's Squadron from Lille Aerodrome. We were somewhere over Menin, and the Hun was still gaining height, though we were both near the tops of our respective ceilings. Not all the enemy aircraft were equipped with machine guns in those early days, but the German observer potted at me from the rear cockpit with a parabellum pistol, and as some of his bullets came unpleasantly close, I thought it high time to retaliate, and gave him a drum from my Lewis gun without much effect. But when I wanted to take off the empty drum and replace it with a full one, it seemed to jam, and as I was unable to remove it with one hand, I wedged the stick between my knees and tugged at the obstinate thing with both hands.

After one of two fruitless efforts, I raised myself up out of my seat in order to get a better grip, and I suppose that my safety belt must have slipped down at the critical moment. Anyhow, my knees loosened their grip on the stick just as the Martynside, which was already climbing at its maximum angle, stalled and flicked over into a spin.

As I was more than half out of the cockpit at the time, the spin threw me clear of the machine, but I still kept both my hands on the drum of the Lewis gun. Only a few seconds previously I had been cursing because I could not get that drum off, but now I prayed fervently that it would stay on for ever.

I knew it might come off any moment, however, and as its edge was cutting my fingers badly, I had to get a firmer hold of something more reliable. The first thing I thought of was the top of the centre section strut, which at that time was behind and below the Lewis gun, but as the machine was now flying upside down, I had sufficient wits left to realise that it was behind and above me, though where it was exactly I could not tell.

Dare I let go the drum with one hand and make a grab for it? Well, there was nothing else for it but to take the risk; I let go and found the strut all right, and then I released my other hand and gripped the strut on the other side. I was then in a more comfortable position, and at least I felt rather more part of my machine than I had done in my original attitude.

My chin was rammed against the top plane, beside the gun, while my legs were waving about in empty air. The Martynside was upside down in a flat spin, and from my precarious position the only thing I could see was the propeller (which seemed unpleasantly close to my face), the town of Menin, and the adjacent countryside. Menin and its environs were revolving at an impossible angle – apparently above me – and getting larger with every turn. I began to wonder what sort of a spot I was going to crash on.

Then I got angry and cursed myself for a fool for wasting time on such idle speculations, while at the same time it dawned on me that my only chance of righting the machine lay in getting my feet into the cockpit. If I could manage it, I knew that I was bound to fall automatically into the cockpit when the machine came over.

I kept on kicking upwards behind me until at last I got first one foot and then the other hooked inside the cockpit. Somehow I got the stick between my legs again, and jammed on full aileron and elevator; I do not know exactly what happened then, but somehow the trick was done. The machine came over the right way up, and I fell off the top plane into my seat with a bump.

I grabbed at the stick with both hands and thanked my lucky stars when I got hold of it. Then to my surprise I found myself unable to move it. I suddenly realised that I was sitting much lower than usual inside the cockpit; in fact, I was so low down that I could not see over the edge at all. On investigation I found that the bump of my fall had sent me right through my seat, with the result that I was sitting on the floor of the machine as well as on the controls, which I was jamming. The cushion had fallen out when the machine turned upside down, along with everything else that was loose or had been kicked loose when I was trying to find the stick with my feet.

Something had to be done quickly, as although the engine had stopped through lack of petrol when the machine was upside down, it was now roaring away merrily and taking me down in a dive which looked likely to end in the wood to the north of Menin. So I throttled back and braced my shoulders against the top of the fuselage, and my feet against the rudder bar; then I pulled out the broken bits of seat and freed the controls. Luckily I found them working all right, so that I was able to put the machine's nose up and open the throttle again. I rose and cleared the trees on the Menin road with very little to spare.

I did not trouble to climb any more, but just flew back along the Menin road. In my efforts to find the control stick with my feet, I had smashed all the instruments on the dashboard, and as I gazed at the damage, I wondered if I could ever make any one realise how it had been done. I had only a very hazy idea myself as to what had really happened, but I felt happy to be alive, and thought it simply marvellous that I was still able to control the machine.

I hurried back to Abeele, without worrying about the increasing strain on the small of my back or the futile shots that the Germans on the ground were sending after me. I went to bed early that night and slept for a good solid twelve hours; but, Lord, how stiff I was the next day! It took a long time before I was able to move about with any comfort.

CHAPTER TWELVE

THE DAY'S WORK

By 'Contact' (Alan Bott)

For weeks we had talked guardedly of 'it' and 'them' ... of the greatest day of the Push and the latest form of warfare. Details of the twin mysteries had been rightly kept secret by the red-hatted Olympians who really knew, though we of the fighting branches had heard sufficient to stimulate an appetite for rumour and exaggeration. Consequently we possessed our souls in impatience and dabbled in conjecture.

Small forts moving on the caterpillar system of traction used for heavy guns were to crawl across No Man's Land, enfilade the enemy front line with quick-firing and machine guns, and hurl bombs on such of the works and emplacements as they did not ram to pieces – thus a confidential adjutant, who seemed to think he had admitted me into the inner circle of knowledge, tenanted only by himself and the GSO people (I, II, and III, besides untabbed nondescripts). Veterans gave tips on war in the open country, or chatted airily about another tour of such places as Le Catelet, Le Cateau, Mons, the Maubeuge district, and Namur. The cautious listened in silence, and distilled only two facts from the dubious mixture of fancy. The first was that we were booked for a big advance one of these fine days; and the second that new armoured cars, caterpillared and powerfully armed, would make their bow to Brother Boche.

The balloon of swollen conjecture floated over the back of the Front until it was destroyed by the quick-fire of authentic orders, which necessarily revealed much of the plan and many of the methods. On the afternoon of 14 September all the officers of our aerodrome were summoned to an empty shed. There we found our own particular General, who said more to the point in five minutes than the rumourists had said in five weeks. There was to be a grand attack next morning. The immediate objectives were not distant, but their gain would be of enormous value. Every atom of energy must be concentrated on the task. It was hoped that an element of surprise would be on our side, helped by a new engine of war christened the Tank. The nature of this strange animal, male and female, was then explained.

Next came an exposition of the part allotted to the Flying Corps. No German machines could be allowed near enough to the lines for any observation. We must shoot all enemy machines at sight and give them no rest. Our bombers should make life a burden on the enemy lines of communication. Infantry and transport were to be worried, whenever possible, by machine gun fire from above. Machines would be detailed for contact work with our infantry. Reconnaissance jobs were to be completed at all costs, if there seemed the slightest chance of bringing back useful information.

No more bubbles of hot air were blown around the mess table. Only the evening was between us and the day of days. The time before dinner was filled by the testing of machines and the writing of those cheerful, non-committal letters that precede big happenings at the front. Our flight had visitors to dinner, but the shadow of tomorrow was too insistent for the racket customary on a guest night. It was as if the electricity had been withdrawn from the atmosphere and condensed for use when required. The dinner talk was curiously re-strained. The usual shop chatter prevailed, leavened by snatches of bantering cynicism from those infants of the world who thought that to be a *beau sabreur* (dashing adventurer) of the air one must juggle verbally with life, death and Archie shells. Even these war babies (three of them died very gallantly before we reassembled for breakfast next day) had bottled most of their exuberance. Understanding silences were sandwiched between yarns. A wag searched for the Pagliacci record, and set the gramophone to churn out 'Vesti la Giubba'. The guests stayed to listen politely to a few revue melodies, and then slipped away. The rest turned in immediately, in view of the jobs at early dawn.

'Night, everybody,' said one of the flight-commanders. 'Meet you at Mossy-Face in the morning!'

In the morning some of us saw him spin earthwards over Mossy-Face Wood, surrounded by German machines.

Long before the dawn of 15 September, I awoke to the roar of engines, followed by an overhead drone as a party of bombers circled round until they were ready to start. When this noise had died away, the dull boom of an intense bombardment was able to make itself heard. I rolled over and went to sleep again, for our own show was not due to start until three hours later.

The Flying Corps programme on the great day was a marvel of organisation. The jobs fitted into one another, and into the general tactical scheme of the advance, as exactly as the parts of a flawless motor. At no time could enemy craft steal toward the lines to spy out the land. Every sector was covered by defensive patrols, which travelled northward and southward, southward and northward, eager to pounce on any black-crossed stranger. Offensive patrols moved and fought over Boche territory until they were relieved by other offensive patrols. The machines on artillery observation were thus worried only by Archie, and the reconnaissance formations were able to do their work with little interruption, except when they passed well outside the patrol areas. Throughout the day those guerrillas of the air, the bombing craft, went across and dropped eggs on anything between general headquarters and a railway line. The corps buses kept constant communication between attacking battalions and the rear. A machine first reported the exploit of the immortal Tank that waddled down High Street, Flers, spitting bullets and inspiring sick fear. And there were many free-lance stunts, such as Lewis gun attacks on reserve troops or on trains.

The three squadrons attached to our aerodrome had to the day's credit two long reconnaissances, three offensive patrols, and four bomb raids. Six enemy machines were destroyed on these shows, and the bombers did magnificent work at vital points. At 2.00am they dropped eggs on the German Somme headquarters. An hour later they deranged the railway station of a large garrison town. For the remaining time before sunset they were not so busy. They merely destroyed an ammunition train, cut two railway lines, damaged an important railhead, and sprayed a bivouac ground.

An orderly called me at 4.15am for the big offensive patrol. The sky was a dark grey curtain decorated by faintly twinkling stars. I dressed to the thunderous accompaniment of the guns, warmed myself with a cup of hot cocoa, donned flying kit, and hurried to the aerodrome. There we gathered around the patrol leader, who gave us final instructions about the method of attack. We tested our guns and climbed into the machines.

By now the east had turned to a light grey, with pink smudges from the forefinger of sunrise. Punctually, at 5 o'clock, the order 'Start up!' passed down the long line of machines. The flight-commander's engine began a loud metallic roar, then softened as it was throttled down. The pilot waved his hand, the chocks were pulled from under the wheels, and the machine moved forward. The throttle was again opened full out as the bus raced into the wind until flying speed had been attained, when it skimmed gently from the ground. We followed, and carried out the rendezvous at 3,000 feet.

The morning light increased every minute, and the grey of the sky was merging into blue. The faint, hovering ground mist was not sufficient to screen our landmarks. The country below was a shadowy patchwork of coloured pieces. The woods, fantastic shapes of dark green, stood out strongly from the mosaic of brown and green fields. The pattern was divided and sub-divided by the straight, poplar-bordered roads peculiar to France.

We passed on to the dirty strip of wilderness that was the actual Front. The battered villages and disorderly ruins looked like hieroglyphics traced on wet sand. A sea of smoke rolled over the ground for miles. It was a by-product of one of the most terrific bombardments in the history of trench warfare. Through it hundreds of gun-flashes twinkled, like the lights of a Chinese garden.

Having reached a height of 12,000 feet, we crossed the trenches south of Bapaume. As the danger that stray bullets might fall on friends no longer existed, pilots and observers fired a few rounds into space to make sure their guns were behaving properly.

Archie began his frightfulness early. He concentrated on the leader's machine, but the still dim light spoiled his aim, and many of the bursts were dotted between the craft behind. I heard the customary *wouff! wouff! wouff!* followed in one case by the *hs-s-s-s-s* of passing fragments. We swerved and dodged to disconcert the gunners. After five minutes of hide-and-seek, we shook off this group of Archie batteries.

The flight-commander headed for Mossy-Face Wood, scene of many air battles and bomb raids. An aerodrome just east of the wood was the home of the Fokker star, Boelcke. The patrol leader led us to it, for it was his great ambition to account for Germany's best pilot.

While we approached, I looked down and saw eight machines with black Maltese crosses on their planes, about 3,000 feet below. They had clipped wings of a peculiar whiteness, and they were ranged one above the other, like the rungs of a Venetian blind. A cluster of small scouts swooped down from Heaven-knows-what height and hovered above us; but our leader evidently did not see them, for he dived steeply on the enemy underneath, accompanied by the two machines nearest him. The other group of enemies then dived.

I looked up and saw a narrow biplane, apparently a Roland, rushing towards our bus. My pilot turned vertically and then side-slipped to disconcert the Boche's aim. The black-crossed craft swept over at a distance of less than 100 yards. I raised my gun-mounting, sighted, and pressed the trigger. Three shots rattled off – and my Lewis gun ceased fire.

Intensely annoyed at being cheated out of such a promising target, I applied immediate action, pulled back the cocking handle, and pressed the trigger again. Nothing happened. After one more immediate action test, I examined the gun and found that an incoming cartridge and an empty case were jammed together in the breech. To remedy the stoppage I had to remove spade-grip and body-cover. As I did this, I heard an ominous *ta-ta-ta-ta-ta* from the returning German scout. My pilot cartwheeled round and made for the German, his gun spitting continuously through the propeller. The two machines raced at each other until less than 50 yards separated them. Then the Boche swayed, turned aside, and put his nose down. We dropped after him, with our front machine gun still speaking. The Roland's glide merged into a dive, and we imitated him. Suddenly a streak of flame came from his petrol tank, and the next second he was rushing earthwards, with two streamers of smoke trailing behind.

I was unable to see the end of this vertical dive, for two more single-seaters were upon us. They plugged away while I remedied the stoppage, and several bullets ventilated the fuselage quite close to my cockpit. When my gun was itself again I changed the drum of ammunition, and hastened to fire at the nearest enemy. He was evidently unprepared, for he turned and moved across our tail. As he did so I raked his bus from stem to stern. I looked at him hopefully, for the range was very short, and I expected to see him drop towards the ground at several miles a minute. He sailed on serenely. This is an annoying habit of enemy machines when one is sure that, by the rules of the game, they ought to be destroyed. The machine in question was probably hit, however, for it did not return, and I saw it begin to glide as though the pilot meant to land. We switched our attention to the remaining German, but this one was not anxious to fight alone. He dived a few hundred feet with tail well up, looking for all the world like a trout when it drops back into water. Afterwards he flattened out and went east.

During the fight we had become separated from the remainder of our party. I searched all-round the compass, but could find neither friend nor foe. We returned to the aerodrome where hostile craft were first sighted. There was no sign of our patrol leader's machine or of the others who dived on the first group of enemy craft. Several German machines were at rest in the aerodrome.

Finding ourselves alone, we passed on towards the lines. I twisted my neck in every direction, for over enemy country only a constant lookout above, below, and on all sides can save a machine from a surprise attack. After a few minutes, we spotted six craft bearing towards us from a great height. Through field-glasses I was able to see their black crosses.

The strangers dived in two lots of three. I waited until the first three were within 300 yards' range and opened fire. One of them swerved away, but the other two passed right under us. Something sang to the right, and I found that part of a landing wire was dangling helplessly from its socket. We thanked whatever gods there be that it was not a flying wire, and turned to meet the next three. We swerved violently, and they pulled out of their dive well away from us. With nose down and engine full out, we raced towards the lines and safety. Three of the attackers were unable to keep up with us and we left them behind.

The other three Germans, classed by our pilot as Halberstadts, had a great deal more speed than ours. They did not attack at close quarters immediately, but flew 200 to 300 yards behind, ready to pounce at their own moment. Two of them got between my gun and our tail-plane, so that they were safe from my fire. The third was slightly above our height, and for his benefit I stood up and rattled through a whole ammunition-drum. Here let me say I do not think I hit him, for he was not in difficulties. He dived below us to join his companions, possibly because he did not like being under fire when they were not. To my surprise and joy, he fell slick on one of the other two enemy machines. This latter broke into two pieces, which whistled downward. The machine responsible for my luck side-slipped, spun a little, recovered, and went down to land. The third made off east.

In plain print and at a normal time, this episode shows little that is comic. But when it happened I was in a state of high tension, and this, combined with the startling realisation that a German pilot had saved me and destroyed his friend seemed irresistibly comic. I cackled with laughter, and was annoyed because my pilot did not see the joke.

We reached the lines without further trouble from anything but Archie. The pink streaks of daybreak had now disappeared beneath the whole body of the sunrise, and the sky was of that intense blue which is the secret of high altitudes. What was left of the ground-mist shimmered as it congealed in the sunlight. The pall of smoke from the guns had doubled in volume. The Ancre sparkled brightly.

We cruised around in a search for others of our party, but found none. A defensive patrol was operating between Albert and the trenches. We joined it for half an hour, at the end of which I heard a 'Halloa!' from the speaking-tube.

'What's up now?' I asked.

'Going to have a look at the war,' was the pilot's reply.

Before I grasped his meaning he had shut off the engine and we were gliding towards the trenches. At 1,200 feet we switched on, flattened out, and looked for movement below. There was no infantry advance at the moment, but below Courcelette what seemed to be two ungainly masses of black slime were slithering over the ground. I rubbed my eyes and looked again. One of them actually crawled among the scrapheaps that fringed the ruins of the village. Only then did the thought that they might be Tanks suggest itself. Afterwards I discovered that this was so.

The machine rocked violently as a projectile hurtled by underneath us. The pilot remembered the broken landing-wire and steered for home. After landing, we compared notes with others who had returned from the expedition. Our leader, we learned, was down at last, after seventeen months of flying on active service, with only one break for any appreciable time. He destroyed one more enemy before the Boches got him. In the dive he got right ahead of the machines that followed him. As these hurried to his assistance, they saw an enemy plane turn over, show a white, gleaming belly, and drop in zig-zags. Our leader's bus was then seen to heel over into a vertical dive and to plunge down, spinning rhythmically on its axis. Probably he was shot dead and fell over on to the joystick, which put the machine to its last dive. The petrol tank of the second machine to arrive among the Germans was plugged by a bullet, and the pilot was forced to land. Weeks later, his observer wrote us a letter from a prison camp in Hanover. The third British bus, perforated by scores of bullet-holes, got back to tell the tale.

Our lost patrol leader was one of the best pilots produced thus far. He was utterly fearless, and had more time over the German lines to his credit than anyone else in the Flying Corps. It was part of his fatalistic creed that Archie should never be dodged, and he would go calmly ahead when the AA guns were at their best. Somehow the bursts never found him. He had won both the DSO and the MC for deeds in the air. Only the evening before, when asked lightly if he was out for a VC, he said he would rather get Boelcke than the VC; and in the end Boelcke probably got him, for he fell over the famous German pilot's aerodrome, and that day the German wireless announced that Boelcke had shot down two more machines. Peace to the ashes of a fine pilot and a very brave man!

Two observers, other than the leader's passenger, had been killed during our patrol. One of them was 'Uncle', a captain in the North-umberland Fusiliers. A bullet entered the large artery of his thigh. He bled profusely and lost consciousness in the middle of a fight with two Boches. When he came to, a few minutes later, he grabbed his gun and opened fire on an enemy. After about forty shots the chatter of the gun ceased, and through the speaking-tube a faint voice told the pilot to look round. The pilot did so, and saw a Maltese-crossed biplane fall-ing in flames. But Uncle had faded into unconsciousness again, and he never came back. It is more than possible that if he had put a tourniquet round his thigh, instead of continuing the fight, he might have lived.

An easy death, you say? One of many such. Only the day before I had helped to lift the limp body of Paddy from the floor of an observer's cockpit. He had been shot over the heart. He fainted, recovered his senses for ten minutes, and kept two enemy craft at bay until he died, by which time the trenches were reached.

Imagine yourself under fire in an aeroplane at 10,000 feet ... that only a second ago you were in the country of shadows. Imagine your-self feeling giddy and deadly sick from loss of blood, and what is left of your consciousness to be stabbed insistently by a throbbing pain. Now imagine how you would force yourself in this condition to grasp a machine gun in your numbed hand, pull back the cocking-handle, take careful aim at a fast machine, allowing for deflection, and fire until you sink into death. Someday I hope to be allowed to visit Valhalla for half an hour that I may congratulate Paddy and Uncle.

We refreshed ourselves with cold baths and hot breakfasts. In the mess the fights were reconstructed. Sudden silences were frequent, an unspoken tribute to the patrol leader and the other casualties. But at lunch-time we were cheered by the news that the first and second objectives had been reached, that Martinpuich, Courcelette and Flers had fallen, and that the Tanks had behaved well.

After lunch I rested awhile before the long reconnaissance, due to start at three. Six machines were detailed for this job; though a faulty engine kept one of them on the ground. The observers marked the course on their maps, and wrote out lists of railway stations. At 3.30pm we set off towards Arras.

Archie hit out as soon as we crossed to his side of the Front. He was especially dangerous that afternoon, as if determined to avenge the German defeat of the morning. Each bus in turn was encircled by black bursts, and each bus in turn lost height, swerved, or changed its course to defeat the gunner's aim. A piece of HE hit our tail plane, and stayed there until I cut it out for a souvenir when we had returned.

The observers were kept busy with note book and pencil, for the train movement was far greater than the average, and streaks of smoke courted attention on all the railways. Rolling stock was correspondingly small, and the counting of the trucks in the sidings was not difficult. Road and canal transport was plentiful. As evidence of the urgency of all this traffic, I remarked that no effort at concealment was made. On ordinary days, a German train always shut off steam when we approached; and I have often seen transport passing along the road one minute, and not passing along the road the next. On 5 September the traffic was too urgent for time to be lost by hide-and-seek.

We passed several of our offensive patrols, each of whom escorted us while we were on their beat. It was curious that no activity could be noticed on the enemy aerodromes. Until we passed Mossy-Face on the last lap of the homeward journey we saw no Boche aircraft. Even there the machines with black crosses flew very low and did not attempt to offer battle.

Nothing out of the ordinary happened until we were about to cross the trenches north of Peronne. Archie then scored an inner. One of his chunks swept the left aileron from the leader's machine, which banked vertically, almost rolled over, and began to spin. For 2,000 feet the irregular drop continued, and the observer gave up hope. Luckily for him the pilot was not of the same mind, and managed to check the spin by juggling with his rudder-controls. The bus flew home, left wing well down, with the observer leaning far out to the right to restore equilibrium, while the icy rush of air boxed his ears.

We landed, wrote our reports, and took them to headquarters. The day's work had been done, which was all that mattered to any extent, and a very able general told us it was 'dom good (*sic*.).' But many a day passed before we grew accustomed to the absence of Uncle and Paddy.

And so to bed, until we were called for another early morning show.

II

It happened late in the afternoon, one August dog-day. No wind leavened the languid air, and hut, hangar, tent, and workshop were oppressive with a heavy heat, so that we wanted to sleep. To taxi across the grass in a chase for flying speed, to soar gently from the hot ground, and, by leaning beyond the windscreen, to let the slip-stream of displaced air play on one's face – all this was refreshing as a cold plunge after a Turkish bath. I congratulated myself that I was no longer a gunner, strenuous over interminable corrections, or tiredly erect in a close observation post.

Our party consisted of four machines, each complete with pilot, observer, and several hundred rounds of ammunition. The job was an offensive patrol, that is to say, we were to hunt trouble around a given area behind the Boche lines. A great deal of the credit for our 'mastery of the air' – that glib phrase of the question-asking politician – during the Somme Push of 1916 belongs to those who organised and those who led these fighting expeditions over enemy country. Thanks to them, our aircraft were able to carry out reconnaissance, artillery observation, and photography with a minimum of interruption, while the German planes were so hard pressed to defend their place in the air that they could seldom guide their own guns or collect useful information. To this satisfactory result must be added the irritative effect on enemy morale of the knowledge that whenever the weather was fine our machines hummed overhead, ready to molest and be molested.

Offensive patrols are well worth while, but for the comfort of those directly concerned they are rather too exciting. When friends are below during an air duel, then should he or his machine be crippled he can break away and land, and there's an end of it. But if a pilot be wounded in a scrap far away from home, before he can land he must fly for many miles, under shell fire and probably pursued by enemies. He must conquer the blighting faintness which accompanies loss of blood, keep clearheaded enough to deal instantaneously with adverse emergency, and make an unwilling brain command unwilling hands and feet to control a delicate apparatus. Worst of all, if his engine be put out of action at a spot beyond gliding distance of the lines, there is nothing for it but to descend and tamely surrender. And always he is within reach of that vindictive exponent of frightfulness, Archibald the Ever-Ready.

As we climbed to 4,000 feet the machines above threw glints of sunlight on the screen of blue infinity. We ranged ourselves and departed. Passing the red roofs and heart-shaped citadel of Doullens and a jagged wood suggestive of a lion rampant, we followed the straight road to Arras. Arrived there, the leader turned south, for we were not yet high enough. As we moved along the brown band of shell-pocked desolation we continued to climb. Patches of smoke from the guns hovered over the ground at intervals. A score of lazy-looking kite balloons hung motionless.

By the time we reached Albert our height was 12,000 feet, and we steered eastward over the ground gained in the June–July advance. Beyond the scrap-heap that once was Pozières two enormous mine craters showed up, dented into the razed surface, one on either side of the Albert-Bapaume road. Flying very low, a few buses were working on trench reconnaissance. The sunshine rebounded from the top of their wings, and against the discoloured earth they looked like fireflies. A mile or so behind the then front lines were the twin villages of Courcelette and Martinpuich, divided only by the road. Already they were badly battered, though, unlike Pozieres, they still deserved the title of village. Le Sars, which sat astride the road, nearer Bapaume, had been set afire by our guns, and was smoking.

In those days, before the methodical advance of the Somme artillery had begun to worry the stronghold overmuch, Bapaume was a hotbed of all the anti-aircraft devilries. We therefore swerved toward the south. Archie was not to be shaken off so easily, and we began a series of erratic deviations as he ringed with black puffs first one machine then another. The shooting was not particularly good; for although no clouds intervened between the guns and their mark, a powerful sun dazzled the gunners, who must have found difficulty in judging height and direction. From Archie's point of view, the perfect sky is one screened from the sunlight, at 20,000 to 30,000 feet, by a mantle of thin clouds against which aircraft are outlined boldly, like stags on a snow-covered slope.

A few minutes in a south-easterly direction brought us to the Bois d'Havrincourt, a large ungainly wood, the shape of which was something between the ace of spades and the ace of clubs. This we knew as

Mossy-Face. The region around it was notorious in RFC messes as being the chief centre of the Boche Flying Corps on the British Front.

From the south-west corner Archie again scattered burst and bark at our group, but his inaccuracy made dodging hardly necessary. A lull followed, and I twisted my neck all-round the compass for, in the presence of hostile aeroplanes, Archie seldom behaves, except when friendly machines are about. Some 2,000 feet below three biplanes were approaching the wood from the south. Black crosses showed up plainly on their grey-white wings. We dropped into a dive toward the strangers.

Under normal conditions a steep dive imparts a feeling of being hemmed in from every side. One takes a deep breath instinctively, and the novice to flying will grip the fuselage, as if to avoid being crushed. And, indeed, a passenger in a diving aeroplane is hemmed in by the terrific air-pressure to which the solid surface is subjected. If he attempts to stand up or lean over the side, he will be swept back, after a short struggle, beneath the shelter of wind-screen and fuselage. But when diving on an enemy, I have never experienced this troubled sensation, probably because it has been swamped under the high tension of readiness for the task. All the faculties must be concentrated on opening the attack, since an air duel is often decided in the first few seconds at close quarters. What happens during these few seconds may depend on a trifle, such as the position of the gun-mounting, an untried drum of ammunition, a slight swerve, or firing a second too soon or too late. An airman should regard his body as part of the machine when there is a prospect of a fight, and his brain, which commands the machine, must be instinctive with insight into what the enemy will attempt.

As we dived, then, I estimated the angle at which we might cross the Boche trio, watched for a change of direction on their part, slewed round the gun-mounting to the most effective setting for what would probably be my arc of fire, and fingered the movable back-sight. At first the enemy held to their course as though quite unconcerned. Later, they began to lose height. Their downward line of flight became steeper and steeper, and so did ours.

Just as our leading bus arrived within range and began to spit bullets through the propeller, a signal rocket streaked from the first Boche biplane, and the trio dived almost vertically, honking the while on Klaxon horns. We were then at about 6,000 feet.

We were expecting to see the enemy flatten out, when 'Wouff! wouff! wouff! wouff! wouff!' said Archie. The German birds were not hawks at all; they were merely tame decoys used to entice us to a pre-arranged spot, at a height well favoured by A-A gunners. The ugly puffs encircled us, and it seemed unlikely that an aeroplane could get away without being caught in a patch of hurtling high explosive. Yet nobody was hit. The only redeeming feature of the villain Archibald is that his deeds are less terrible than his noise, and even this is too flat to be truly frightful. Although I was uncomfortable as we raced away, the chorused *wouffs!* reminded me of an epidemic of coughing I heard in church one winter's Sunday while a sermon was read by a dull-voiced vicar.

Mingled with the many black bursts were a few green ones, probably gas shells, for Archie had begun to experiment with the gas habit. Very suddenly a line of fiery rectangles shot up and curved towards us when they had reached three-quarters of their maximum height. They rose and fell within 30 yards of our tail. These were 'onions', the flaming rockets which the Boche keeps for any hostile aircraft that can be lured to a height between 4,000 and 6,000 feet.

I yelled to my pilot that we should have to dodge. We side-slipped and swerved to the left. A minute later the stream of onions had disappeared, greatly to my relief, for the prospect of a fire in the air inspires in me a mortal funk. Soon we were to pass from the unpleasant possibility to the far more unpleasant reality.

Once outside the unhealthy region, we climbed to a less dangerous height. Again we became the target for a few dozen HE shells. We broke away and swooped downward. Some little distance ahead, and not far below, was a group of five Albatross two-seaters. Our machine was pointed at them, in the wake of the flight-commander's bus.

Next instant the fuselage shivered. I looked along the inside of it and found that a burning shell fragment was lodged on a longeron, half-way between my cockpit and the tail-plane. A little game zig-zagged over the fabric, all but died away, but, being fanned by the wind as we lost height, recovered and licked its way toward the tail. I was too far away to reach the flame with my hands, and the fire extinguisher was by the pilot's seat. I called for it into the speaking-tube. The pilot made no move. Once more I shouted. Again no answer. The pilot's earpiece had slipped from under his cap. A thrill of acute fear passed through me as I stood up, forced my arm through the rush of wind, and grabbed his shoulder.

'Fuselage burning! Pass the fire extinguisher!' I yelled.

My words were drowned in the engine's roar; and the pilot, intent on getting near the Germans, thought I had asked which one we were to attack.

'Look out for those two Boches on the left,' he called over his shoulder.

'Pass the fire extinguisher!'

'Get ready to shoot, blast you!'

'Fire extinguisher, you ruddy fool!'

A backward glance told me that the fire was nearing the tailplane at the one end and my box of ammunition at the other, and was too serious for treatment by the extinguisher unless I could get it at once. Desperately I tried to force myself through the bracing struts and cross-wires behind my seat. To my surprise, head and shoulders and one arm got to the other side – a curious circumstance, as afterwards I tried repeatedly to repeat this contortionist trick on the ground, but failed every time. There I stuck, for it was impossible to wriggle farther. However, I could now reach part of the fire, and at it I beat with gloved hands. Within half a minute most of the fire was crushed to death. But a thin streak of flame, outside the radius of my arm, still flickered towards the tail. I tore off one of my gauntlets and swung it furiously on to the burning strip. The flame lessened, rose again when I raised the glove, but died out altogether after I had hit it twice more. The load of fear left me, and I discovered an intense discomfort, wedged in as I was between the two crossed bracing-struts. Five minutes passed before I was able, with many a heave and gasp, to withdraw back to my seat.

By now we were at close grips with the enemy, and our machine and another converged on an enemy. All shot industriously. As we turned, my pilot glared at me, and knowing nothing of the fire, shouted: 'Why the hell haven't you fired yet?' I caught sight of a Boche bus below us, aimed at it, and emptied a drum in short bursts. It swept away, but not before two of the German observer's bullets had plugged our petrol tank from underneath. The pressure went, and with it the petrol supply. The needle on the rev-counter quivered to the left as the revolutions dropped, and the engine missed on first one, then two cylinders. We turned round, and, with nose down, headed for the trenches. just then the engine ceased work altogether, and we began to glide down.

All this happened so quickly that I had scarcely realised our plight. Next I began to calculate our chances of reaching the lines before we would have to land. Our height was 9,000 feet, and we were just over 9½ miles from friendly territory. Reckoning the gliding possibilities of our type of bus as 1 mile to 1,000 feet, the odds seemed unfavourable. On the other hand, a useful wind had arisen from the east, and a very skilful pilot would certainly cover all the distance that could be covered.

I located our exact position and searched the map for the nearest spot in the lines. The village of Bouchavesnes was a fraction south of due west, and I remembered that the French had stormed it two days previously. From the shape of the line before this advance, there was evidently a small salient, with Bouchavesnes in the middle of the curve. I scribbled this observation on a scrap of paper, which I handed to the pilot with the compass direction. He checked up on the map, nodded over his shoulder, and set a course for Bouchavesnes.

Could we do it? I prayed to the gods and trusted to the pilot. Through my mind there flitted impossible plans to be tried if we landed in Boche territory. After setting fire to the machine we would attempt to hide, and then, at night-time, creep along a communication trench to the enemy front line, jump across it in a gap between the sentries, and chance getting by the barbed wire and across No Man's Land. Or we would steal to the Somme, float downstream, and somehow or other pass the entanglements placed across the river by the enemy. *Wouff! wouff!* Archie was complicating the odds.

Further broodings were checked by the sudden appearance of a German scout. Taking advantage of our plight, its pilot dived steeply from a point slightly behind us. We could not afford to lose any distance by dodging, so we did the only thing possible – we kept straight on. I raised my gun, aimed at the wicked-looking nose of the attacking craft, and met it with a barrage of bullets. These must have worried the Boche, for he swerved aside when 150 yards distant, and did not flatten out until he was beneath the tail of our machine. Afterwards he climbed away from us, turned, and dived once more. For a second time we escaped, owing either to some lucky shots from my gun or to the lack of judgment by the enemy pilot. The scout pulled up and passed ahead of us. It rose and manoeuvred as if to dive from the front and bar the way.

Meanwhile, four specks, approaching from the west, had grown larger and larger, until they were revealed as of the FE type – the

British 'pusher' two-seater. The Boche saw them, and hesitated as they bore down on him. Finding himself in the position of a lion attacked by hunters when about to pounce on a tethered goat, he decided not to destroy, for in so doing he would have laid himself open to destruction. When I last saw him he was racing north-east.

There was now no obstacle to the long glide. As we went lower, the torn ground showed up plainly. From 2,000 feet I could almost count the shell-holes. Two battery positions came into view, and near one of them I saw tracks and could distinguish movement by a few tiny dots. It became evident that, barring accident, we should reach the French zone.

When slightly behind the trenches a confused chatter from below told us that machine guns were trained on the machine. By way of retaliation, I leaned over and shot at what looked like an emplacement. Then came the Boche front line, ragged and unkempt. I fired along the open trench. Although far from fearless, as a rule, I was not in the least afraid during the eventful glide. My state of intense 'wind-up' while the fuselage was burning had apparently exhausted my stock of nervousness. I seemed detached from all idea of danger, and the desolated German trench area might have been a side-show at a fair.

We swept by No Man's Land at a height of 600 feet, crossed the French first and second-line trenches, and, after passing a small ridge, prepared to land on an uneven plateau covered by high bracken. To avoid landing down wind and down-hill; the pilot banked to the right before he flattened out. The bus pancaked gently to earth, ran over the bracken, and stopped 2 yards from a group of shell-holes. Not a wire was broken. The propeller had been scored by the bracken, but the landing was responsible for no other damage. Taking into consideration the broken ground, the short space, and the fact that we landed cross-wind, the pilot had exhibited wonderful skill.

We climbed out, relieved but cantankerous. The pilot, still ignorant of the fire, wanted to know why my gun was silent during our first fight; and I wanted to know why he hadn't shut off the engine and listened when I shouted for the fire extinguisher. Some French gunners ran to meet us. The sight that met them must have seemed novel, even to a poilu of two years' understanding.

Supposing that the aeroplane had crashed, they came to see if we were dead or injured. What they found was one almost complete aeroplane and two leather-coated figures, who cursed each other heartily as they stood side by side and performed a natural function which is publicly represented in Brussels by a famous little statue.

'Quels types!' said the first Frenchmen to arrive.

An examination of the bus revealed a fair crop of bullet holes through the wings and elevator. A large gap in one side of the fuselage, over a longeron that was charred to powder in parts, bore witness to the fire. Petrol was dripping from the spot where the tank had been perforated. On taking a tin of chocolate from his pocket, the pilot found it ripped open. He searched the pocket and discovered a bright bullet at the bottom. We traced the adventures of that bullet; it had grazed a strut, cut right through the petrol union, and expended itself on the chocolate tin.

Soon our attention was attracted to several French machines that were passing through a barrage of Archie bursts. The bombardment of an aeroplane arouses only the sporting instinct of the average soldier. His interest, though keen, is directed towards the quality of the shooting and the distance of the shells from their target; his attitude when watching a pigeon-shoot would be much the same. But the airman has experience of what the aeroplane crews must be going through, and his thought is all for them. He knows that dull, loud cough of an Archie shell, the hiss of a flying fragment, the wicked black puffs that creep towards their mark and follow it, no matter where the pilot may swerve. Should a friendly machine tumble to earth after that rare occurrence, a direct hit, all the sensations of an uncontrolled nose-dive are suggested to his senses. He hears the shriek of the up-rushing air, feels the helpless terror. It hurts him to know that he is powerless to save a friend from certain death. He cannot even withdraw his eyes from the falling craft. I was glad we had not viewed the disaster while we were in the air, for nothing is more unnerving than to see another machine crumbled up by a direct hit when Archie is firing at yourself.

'Me,' said a French gunner by my side, 'I prefer the artillery.' With which sentiment I have often agreed when dodging Archie, though at every other time I prefer the Flying Corps work to any other kind of fighting.

The pilot went to phone the Squadron Commander, and I was left with the crippled bus and the crowd of Frenchmen. The poilus questioned me on subjects ranging from the customary length of a British officer's moustache to the possible length of the war. Yes, we had been hit in a fight with Boche aeroplanes, Yes, there had also been a slight fire on board. Yes, I had great fear at the time. Yes, I would accept a cigarette with pleasure. No, it was untrue that England contained 4 million civilian *embusques* (a man of military age who avoids military conscription by obtaining a government job). No, the report that officers of the British Flying Corps received 50 francs a day was inaccurate, unfortunately. But no, my good-for-nothing opinion was that we should not finish the Boche within a year; and so on.

'How is it,' said one man in faded uniform, 'that the British always manage to keep themselves correct and shaven?'

'La barbe!' interrupted another; 'the Tommies don't keep clean on the Somme. Even the lilies of the état-majeur can't.' And he began to quote:

Si ma fi-fi-fiancée me voyait,
Elle m'dirait en me donnant cinq sous:
'Va t' faire raser!' mais moi, j'répondrais
Que moi j'ai toujours les ménes deux joues.

The pilot was away for an hour, and when he did return it was to announce that he had been unable to phone because the line was blocked under the pressure of important operations. Deciding to report in person, we declined an offer of hospitality from the French officers, but gratefully accepted a guard for the machine, and the loan of a car.

A young lieutenant accompanied us as far as Amiens. There we stopped for supper, and were joined by some civilian friends of our French companion. The filet de sole au vin blanc engendered a feeling of deep content. Now that it was over, I felt pleased with the day's excitement and the contrast it afforded. Three hours beforehand it seemed likely that the evening would see us prisoners. Yet here we were, supping in a comfortable hotel with three charming ladies and the widow Clicquot (drinking Champagne – Veuve Cliquot).

Arrived at the aerodrome, we visited the hut of the Squadron Commander, who wore rose-red pyjamas and a smile of welcome. We were just in time, he said, to rescue our names from the list of missing. Our tale impressed him enough to make him say, after making arrangements for the stranded bus to be brought back by a repair party: 'You can both have a rest tomorrow.'

'Blast you and your night-life!' said my tent companion, and mentioned in a hurt tone that our flight was booked for the 5.00am reconnaissance. But my last thought before sinking into sleep was of the blessed words: 'You can have a rest tomorrow.'

INDEX